The Rocking Chair Reader

Coming Home

True Inspirational Tales of Family and Community

Edited by Helen Kay Polaski

Adams Media
Avon, Massachusetts

Published by
Adams Media, an F+W Publications Company
57 Littlefield Street, Avon, MA 02322. U.S.A.
www.adamsmedia.com and *www.rockingchairreader.com*

ISBN: 1-59337-194-2

Printed in the United States of America.

J I H G F E D C B A

Library of Congress Cataloging-in-Publication Data
The rocking chair reader : coming home / [compiled by] Helen Kay Polaski.
p.   cm.
ISBN 1-59337-194-2
1. United States—Biography. 2. United States—Social life and customs.
3. Home—United States. 4. Place (Philosophy) I. Polaski, Helen Kay.
CT215.R63 2004
920.073—dc22
2004003063

Interior illustrations by Roberta A. Ridolfi.
Interior photographs copyright ©2001 Brand X Pictures.

*This book is available at quantity discounts for bulk purchases.
For information, call 1-800-872-5627.*

*This book is dedicated to
small towns everywhere,*

*and to those who keep
the hearth fires burning*

*so the rest of us can
always come home.*

Contents

Acknowledgments

BECAUSE I FIRMLY BELIEVE that everything happens for a reason, I bow my head to the Lord, for it is He who laid this job in my lap.

I am amazed at all the hard work that went into creating this book, and I am so proud to have been part of the team that accomplished the task. I will forever be grateful to Donna Henes for introducing me to Deirdre Mullane, who has been a wonderful agent—thank you for everything, Deirdre!—and also to the entire staff at Adams Media, especially Gary Krebs and Kate Epstein, for choosing me to represent this book, and for being there to smooth out the rough edges.

To the Southeastern Michigan Writers' Association: thank you for all of the pats on the back and for the support throughout this project. To all the talented writers who were courageous enough to submit their work: thank you from the bottom of my heart. Never stop believing in yourself and never stop submitting. Thank you, also, to the dedicated individuals who helped organize the town profiles, and assisted in other ways: Terry Andrew, Dennis Burgess,

Karen Christian-Smith, Barbara A. Davey, Joanne Hulbert, David W. Kendall, Eileen Morris, Bob Rose, Ron Rickabaugh, Melvin Shelly, and Pauline Walters. Thank you so much for jumping in with both feet and helping me uncover such interesting and intimate facts about your hometowns. Some day, I hope to visit each and every one of them.

To my husband and three children: you're the best. Thank you for recognizing how important this project was to me and for giving me the space I needed. To my parents, Harry and Stella Szymanski, and all fifteen of my siblings: thank you for providing me with the understanding of what coming home to a small town really means.

To our Readers: thank you for your support. I believe with all of my heart that you will enjoy *Coming Home* as much as we do.

Introduction

DOROTHY WAS RIGHT. There really is no place like home. Whether you're six years old or eighty, it is virtually impossible to hear the word *home* without feeling powerful emotion.

For some, thoughts of returning home might bring to mind the aroma of their mother's freshly baked bread, or the reassuring safety of their father's arms. For others, a sense of peacefulness might surface, and with it a longing to return to better times. Others may remember home with a smile as they relive childhood memories and secrets between siblings . . . roasting marshmallows over an open fire in the backyard . . . late-afternoon strolls with the neighborhood children . . . promises made . . . love found and lost, only to be found again . . . and the open arms of the special people we can't live without.

For me, home is a tiny cinder-block house in the middle of a small town in Michigan's Lower Peninsula. Times were tough in the '50s; families in our area didn't have much. But my siblings and I grew up feeling quite rich. We had each other and we had a place to call home—in our minds we had everything.

These days when I think of home, I realize much has changed, but at the same time nothing has changed. I feel fortunate to have discovered and clung to one very important concept throughout my life: home will always be home, and sometimes *coming home* is all that matters in the whole world. Of a certainty, home is where the heart is and that will never change. And on those tough days when I feel most vulnerable and find it is impossible to break away and physically return, I take advantage of anything I can get my hands on that can bring home to me, and that, dear Readers, is where this book comes in.

The Rocking Chair Reader series was created to give you the opportunity to return home in just the time it takes to read a short story. The talented authors whose work is included in *Coming Home,* the flagship book of our new series, invite you to come home with them. Though their stories may be different from yours, we feel confident they will jog your memory and similar adventures from your own life will spring forth, bringing the glow that comes only from returning home.

If, like me, you need to be rejuvenated from time to time, look no further. Nestle into your favorite chair, and let *The Rocking Chair Reader* take you home.

Helen Kay Polaski

The Redbirds

by Sandy Williams Driver | *Albertville, Alabama*

MY OLDEST SISTER LEFT HOME in October 1969, when she was just eighteen years old, to join her husband in Alaska. Brenda and Jimmy, high school sweethearts, had married six months earlier. They were hardly back from their honeymoon when the dreaded envelope arrived in the mail: the official draft notice.

Due to Jimmy's excellent typing skills, he received his orders to report for office duty in Alaska immediately after basic training. The forty-ninth state seemed a million miles away from our hometown of Albertville, Alabama, but compared to the raging conflict in Vietnam, the snow and ice sounded just fine. He left for the frigid state in August and sent a ticket for Brenda to join him two months later.

I was three years old that breezy fall day when I watched my sister board the gigantic airplane that would take her farther away from our small southern town than any of us had ever traveled before. Tears ran down Momma's face while Daddy turned away and wiped his misty eyes with a white handkerchief. I waved and waved as that airplane soared out of sight, and although I couldn't see Brenda returning my gesture, I knew she was.

During the days that followed, every time I stepped outside and heard the roar of a jet overhead, I jumped up and down, yelling, "It's Brenda!" I kept my arm in the air until all traces of the plane disappeared from sight and then went to bed happy that night to have seen the aircraft transporting my sister. It never entered my young head that there was more than one airplane in the world. In my toddler eyes Brenda was still a passenger of the friendly skies circling the clouds above my head.

About a week after my sister left, our postman, Mr. Mabry, rang the front bell and hand delivered an envelope covered in funny-looking stamps. It was our first letter from Alaska. Momma read it at least fifty times that afternoon. I liked the last part the best because it contained some very important words especially for me: *Tell Sandy that every time she sees a redbird, I'll be thinking of her.*

Brenda and I loved anything red, especially the scarlet-colored birds often seen fluttering about in our shaded backyard. I was ecstatic when I rushed out the back door and a stately cardinal flew right past my smiling face and perched atop a glider underneath a large pine tree. Surely, Brenda had sent it straight from her new home to let me know I wasn't forgotten.

Mr. Mabry came often to our door, personally delivering every correspondence my sister sent to us. He had once been in the military and knew how important those letters were to a waiting family. In my innocence, I had no idea how the mail system worked and really believed our devoted carrier traveled to Alaska each week to place our letters in my sister's hand and bring hers back to us.

"Please take me with you," I begged on more than one occasion. He just shook his head and said it was too cold up there for me, and besides, his boss wouldn't allow passengers in the mail truck. I was disappointed, but still thrilled when he promised to give Brenda my envelope covered in childish scribbling and rudimentary drawings of stick birds colored a deep crimson.

I saw many redbirds while my sister was gone and I talked to the ones close enough to hear my wishes. I whispered, begging them to fly back and ask my favorite sibling how much longer she was going to be away. I desperately wanted her to return home because she had been my best friend for as long as I could remember and her absence left a hole in my heart that couldn't be filled by anyone else.

I will never forget that day in May 1971 when a whole family of redbirds filled the dogwood tree in our yard. I stood under the blooming branches and couldn't help thinking that Brenda must be trying to tell me something. I rushed into the house and skidded to a stop as I entered the kitchen.

Momma was crying and sobbing loudly. I knew whatever it was that made her shed that many tears had to be pretty bad. Fearing the worst, I wrapped my arms around her waist and held on tight, bracing myself for the impending disaster.

"She's coming home, Sandy. Your sister is coming home," she said in broken sobs.

I knew it! Brenda *was* trying to send a message to me! She had sent the flock of redbirds all the way from Alaska to Alabama to let me know she would be returning soon.

Excitedly, I marked the days off with a big X on the calendar hanging in the den. The night before her scheduled arrival, my excitement was so great I could barely sleep.

For the rest of my life, I will never forget that beautiful summer day when the burgundy 1967 Pontiac GTO pulled into our gravel driveway. The sun was shining and redbirds seemed to be everywhere when Brenda knelt down and gathered me into her arms. I held on tight and vowed to never let her go again.

Thirty-two years later, my sister and I live about three miles apart, high atop beautiful Sand Mountain, in the same town where we were born and raised. We talk on the phone daily, visit often, and still send our love to each other through the redbirds. ❧

The Town of
Albertville, Alabama

Population: 17,000

History: Townsfolk Rally
When the Going Gets Rough

I n 1905, two fires, several months apart, nearly destroyed Albertville. Several years later, disaster befell the small town again when the largest cyclone to ever touch down in Alabama wreaked havoc on Albertville, destroying 250 homes. But Albertville folk could not be held down for long. As the editor of the local newspaper, *The Marshall Banner,* stated: "Disasters retard but can never stop our progress. We are a community of optimists." The townspeople rallied together, rebuilt their homes, and brought their town back to the state it had been in prior to the cyclone's destruction. And as the saying goes, "the proof is in the pudding," for today, Albertville is one of the largest towns on Sand Mountain.

Town Facts

First incorporated: Named after Thomas Albert, Albertville was incorporated on February 18, 1891, with W. M. Coleman serving as first mayor.

Transportation: The primary source of transportation is automotive. The train made its last stop in Albertville in 1946.

Location: Located in northeastern Alabama, Albertville is approximately sixty miles northeast of Birmingham and forty miles southeast of Huntsville.

Places of note: Albertville boasts a manicured pre–Civil War cemetery and a recently renovated downtown area.

Industry: The Fire Hydrant Capital of the World

Fire hydrants—Mueller, the world's largest fire hydrant manufacturer, has operated its factory in Albertville since 1975. The company now produces 550 hydrants a day. Albertville is known as the fire hydrant capital of the world.

Paper plates—The Chinet Co.

Rubber gaskets—Flurocarbon Reeves Rubber Division

Processed steel—Progress Rail

Cotton textiles—Tyco

Steel castings and hubs—Webb Wheel Products

Lumber—Bowater operates a saw mill in Albertville

Poultry—Arbor Acres Farms, Hudson Foods, Tyson, and Wayne Poultry

The Macramé Curtains

by Linda Henson | *Mazon, Illinois*

As I straightened the pillows on my faded green sofa, I noticed another rip. I had already made new covers for the loose cushions, now the permanent cushions on the back were beginning to go. We couldn't afford to have it reupholstered, and we certainly couldn't afford a new one. But there was no time to fret over it now; the women's group at the church was about to begin.

My husband had been the pastor of the church for three years, just enough time for a pastor's family to feel really comfortable in a church. Small towns in central Illinois are quiet and everyone knows everyone else. Mazon was no different. One-tenth of the population attended our church, and during our tenure I learned much about our community.

I didn't especially enjoy the women's group meetings. It was so easy for some of the ladies to fall into gossip that I had become an expert at responding with nonverbal grunts and sighs that neither agreed with negative comments nor reprimanded the gossiper. Changing the subject was my favorite way of dealing with the situation.

Today I changed the subject by asking, "Does anyone have any creative ways of covering up a worn sofa?" My question turned the gossipers into sofa experts and I ended up with a wealth of ideas. An hour and a half later, the president declared the meeting over and directed us toward the desserts.

With cherry cheesecake on a crystal plate decorated with a lace doily, and coffee in a china cup, I was ready to reward myself for avoiding the day's gossip with such finesse when Sue Chambers sat down beside me. Sue, a woman my father would have described as "a bit high-strung," was married to the local doctor. They lived just down the street from our parsonage in a pristine English Tudor with ivy growing up the walls. They were the only people I knew who hired a gardener.

Sue seemed particularly agitated. Apparently, the decorator who had done their home had put curtains in the small windows on each side of their front door, but Sue hadn't checked the fiber content before washing them and the curtains had shrunk to nearly half their original size.

"What will I do?" she asked. "I can't tell my friends how stupid I was. That decorator has moved and I'll never be able to replace them. I'm so upset."

The '70s was the height of the macramé era and I was a macramé queen, so I casually commented that natural macramé hangings would look great in her windows. I added that I'd be glad to do them for her. I hadn't expected her to accept my offer, but to my surprise she called the next day and asked if I had been serious. Panic set in. Would I do a good enough job for a house that had been decorated by a professional? Setting aside my fears, I went to work and the curtains were finished and hung within the week. Sue was thrilled.

Two weeks later, the Victorian doorbell of our antiquated home rang and there stood Sue. She was not the type of person to just drop in for a visit, so my mind raced. Did the curtains fall? Did her husband object? Smiling, she pulled out the package she was holding behind her back and handed it to me.

"I just wanted to truly thank you for the curtains."

I protested, telling her that I enjoyed making the curtains for her and wanted nothing in return, but instead of listening to me she pulled out a card and asked me to read it. As I read, tears stung my eyes.

Everyone thinks because we're the doctor's family and have a little money, we don't need anything. No one has ever done anything for me. You gave me more than curtains.

When I had finished, I leaned over and hugged her. The note was all the thanks I needed.

"Now, look in the bag!" she said excitedly.

I stuck my hand in the bag and pulled out a Gucci purse. Wow! I had never had a designer purse!

Sue seemed more excited than I. Like a little girl passing out Christmas presents, she cried, "Open the purse and look inside!"

I began to pull one thing after another out of the purse: perfume from France, a handkerchief from Switzerland, and a tiny 100-year-old book of prayers that had been purchased in an antique shop in London. After pulling out the last treasure, I was speechless. All I could say was, "You shouldn't have."

A frown crossed her face. "Did you check the bottom?"

There was more? I thought I had emptied it, but there in the bottom of the purse was a roll of bills! I unrolled them and counted five $100 bills! Tears welled up in my eyes again. This was too much. I held the money out to her. "I really don't want to be paid for doing something for you."

Quietly, she pushed my hand away and replied, "I heard you say that you needed a new sofa, and I want to do that for you."

The fact that she had remembered my aging sofa caused more tears to cascade down my cheeks.

Last summer I received an invitation to return to that little town in Illinois to speak at a reunion. As I drove around the town square I was amazed that twenty-five years hadn't changed things very much. It was as if time had bypassed this community. My mind went back to Sue Chambers and I couldn't resist the urge to drive down the block to her ivy-covered home. When I pulled into the drive, tears began to flow. There, on each side of the door, were the little windows still covered with the macramé curtains. ⁊

A Special Cup of Coffee

by Wade A. Stevenson | *Ancell (now Scott City), Missouri*

SEVERAL YEARS AGO, while I was a special agent with a U.S. federal law enforcement agency, I stopped at a McDonald's restaurant just off Highway 61 (now I-55) in southeast Missouri, very near my hometown of Scott City, Missouri. (When I left home in 1955, the population had been approximately 300 and the name of the town had been Ancell.) The memory that ensued made such an impression on me that I made a journal entry recording the story, and have since read and reread it during times in my life when my soul needed uplifting.

Early on that foggy, drizzly morning—just a little past daybreak—I was on an investigation, traveling I-55 near Scott City, when I saw a warm, welcoming McDonald's sign and pulled in for a cup of coffee. The fast-food restaurant was jam-packed; I could barely hear myself speak when placing my order. The high volume of noise was due to the loud din of conversations, and an overhead corner TV that blared information about local basketball playoffs. Most of the customers appeared to be farmers. They milled about in their John Deere and Co-op caps discussing much-needed rain and the basketball playoffs, joking, laughing, and shouting to be heard. That particular Golden Arches stop was obviously a popular gathering place for the neighborhood's friendly early-rising community members. Unfortunately, I saw no one I recognized from my past.

Finding a single table off in a corner, I sat down to have my coffee. I was glancing at the local paper when an even louder noise grabbed my attention. I looked around to see a small boy pushing a child's high chair past me. The casters on the chair made a harsh racket rolling over the tiled floor as he made his way to the only vacant table left in the restaurant. His mother, carrying a tiny baby wrapped in a blanket, was followed by the father. The family sat down and the little boy asked, "I can pray?"

The father smiled and nodded.

Immediately, the room quieted. A pin dropping to the floor could have been heard throughout the restaurant. All discussions, joking, and laughter stopped. The TV was silenced and head apparel promptly removed. The entire restaurant was hushed—the only sound was the precious child's voice raised in prayer. After a long list of "Thank yous," he asked God to bless and keep his mommy, daddy, baby sister, grandma, and pa. Then his sweet, innocent voice whispered, "Amen."

Long moments after the prayer ended, there remained an extended and respectful silence. Curious, I raised my bowed head and looked around. It was apparent to me that in addition to our Dear God, to whom the prayer was specifically addressed, everyone in the restaurant had heard and was touched by the little boy and his prayer. To an individual, everyone wore a warm and proud smile. Some, so moved by this heart-warming scene, reminiscent of one of Norman Rockwell's finest paintings, shed tears. I was one of those and felt proud to be back home again where hearing a child's prayer was far more important than all the other conversations or newscasts. ୭ଚ

Last Leg of the Journey

by Suzanne LaFetra | *Carthage, Indiana*

AFTER HE GOT THE CANCER DIAGNOSIS, my grandfather turned to the woman he'd been married to for fifty-nine years and said, "Lois, let's take a road trip." Clyde Henley had grown up on a farm in Carthage, Indiana. When he talked about home, he tilted his head, as if he could hear the creak of the front-porch steps and the muddy hogs that grunted as the sun went down.

As the shadows slanted toward the horizon and Southern California cooled, my grandparents began their final vacation together to visit a lifetime's accumulation of friends and relatives, and to see the family farm one last time.

After an emotional week in Indiana, they drove to their daughter's Pennsylvania home. But while there, my grandpa slipped and tumbled down the stairs. With both arms encased in plaster, he lay in the house his son-in-law had built, watching the leaves turn yellow, then red, and then brown.

When Grandma called with the news, my eyes drifted around the studio apartment filled with unpacked boxes and I heard myself say, "I'll drive you home, Grandma." I had just split up with my boyfriend of four years and it would do me good to care for someone else, to stop brooding and licking my own wounds. "Yep, Grandma, I love you too," I said as I hung up the phone.

I spent the next nineteen days behind the wheel of my grand-parents' beige '78 Cutlass. Before long, I had settled into the slow pace of our journey, and into the rhythm of my grandparents. We never broke the speed limit and we only drove in daylight. Rarely did we take the main interstate; my grandparents sat in the back chatting and gazing at the clouds as we cruised through small towns, traveling no more than forty-five miles per hour.

Outside a one-hour photo place near Pontiac, we poured over the pictures of their Carthage visit: the cemetery where our ancestors were buried, the framed parchment at city hall bearing my great-great-grandfather's signature, the rusted iron bell at the Henley homestead. They had picnicked with relatives in front of the old barn until the fireflies lit the soft autumn air. My grandpa's voice cracked as he passed me three smooth wooden pegs that had been used in the old barn's construction. I held them in my palm and my mind filled with the squeaking of the horses' leather harnesses and the warm scent of hay.

At a gas station in Bourbon, Missouri, Grandpa grabbed a small spiral notebook from the glove box to record the mileage and what it cost to fill the tank.

"Oh, Grandpa, why are you still keeping track of that stuff?" I asked.

He looked me in the eye and smiled, "Because I've been doing it for forty years." Then, he replaced the log, climbed into the back-seat, and finished the leftover sandwich he'd saved from lunch.

As we eased our way west, the flat black earth stretched around us, tired farmland resting before the next planting. "Tell me again about when you met Grandma at Purdue," I said, looking at him in the rearview mirror and rolling up my window.

At a Howard Johnson's in Plainville, Kansas, my grandparents kissed, and he held her in his plaster-covered arms. At a rest stop, she unbuckled his seat belt for him. He told his stories loudly so that she didn't have to adjust her hearing aid, and she read snippets of the newspaper to us while I drove. He talked of many things, including his days as a home-front soldier in Muskogee. His voice full of humor he'd say, "The only place where you can be in mud up to your knees and have dust blowing in your face."

As autumn unfolded, we saw gleaming grain silos and white-bellied geese that bisected the sky. My grandfather was dealing with the mortality that was racing toward him faster than the asphalt under our tires. My own troubles faded, and each morning as I laced up my running shoes, I breathed in the crisp air and felt increasingly satisfied.

"What'll it be, folks?" the waitress asked, pulling a pencil from her beehive hairdo. My grandfather clumsily unfolded his paper napkin and ordered the same thing he'd ordered every day for the past three days, "A pork loin sandwich."

The Henleys had been hog farmers, and Grandpa loved a good pork loin—the kind you can only get in the Midwest, he always said. I wanted to grant him this small wish, so each day I flipped through the yellow pages at gas stations and called restaurants in towns a few hours ahead of us, searching for eateries that served the sacred sandwiches. But today when he bit into the white bread, I knew something was wrong, just as there had been something amiss with all the others. He sighed as he chewed and I felt like I'd failed again. It must've shown, because Grandma reached across the table and patted my arm. "Honey, the one he wants doesn't exist. He wants the pork loin sandwich made by his mother in 1927."

The sweet smell of cut grass floated through the windows, probably the last trim of the season. We rolled by a sign with a flag that read, "Salute It, Don't Burn It." I yawned as the warm afternoon sun streamed through the windshield, and we stopped in Joplin, Texas, for coffee and orange cupcakes. My grandparents held hands across the speckled Formica table, and their ability to cope with the imminent end to their marriage moved me. I felt honored to witness their strength.

On November second we left Kingman, Arizona. The last leg of the journey, I thought, surveying the sagebrush and beginnings of cactus. On my morning run I lost an earring that my ex-boyfriend had given me, but it didn't seem to matter so much anymore.

At dusk, we pulled into the driveway of my grandparents' butter-colored house, which was surrounded by an unruly lawn and roses in a paint box of colors. I helped Grandpa settle into his bed, and tucked his Purdue blanket around his legs. The rough, mustard-colored wool was frayed from decades of use, but still warm as ever. The photos and mementos from their last visit to Grandpa's birthplace were clustered on his bedside table to keep him company. And those memories, along with those we made on our trip, were tucked in with him clear through to the end of his journey. ᥫ᭡

A Dad and a Dog

by Arthur Bowler | *Randolph, Massachusetts*

ONE PARTICULAR DAY IN 1963 was a tough one for me. It wasn't the local bullies this time, nor the girl next door who wouldn't wear my dime-store ring. Rather, it was an event that plunged a boy, a home-town, and a whole nation into a state of shock, and it was family and community that provided comfort. A small reminder of that day is still with me, and has often helped me through hard times. And in case of fire, I have specific instructions to follow.

On November 22, 1963, I saw a certain look in the eyes of the adults around me, which I had never seen before, and it frightened me. School was let out early in the afternoon and I returned home to a different world, a world that had lost some of its innocence, and a country that seemed to stop in its tracks. Gone were The Four Seasons and The Beach Boys on the radio, replaced with sorrowful music. Where lighthearted TV shows like *I Love Lucy* once entertained us, solemn-faced men announced the latest details of President Kennedy's assassination. Our country, along with one particular parent and child, seemed to be searching for something to hold on to.

Quite spontaneously, Dad asked, "Hey Sport, will you come

downtown with me?" So we walked down Main Street in Randolph, Massachusetts, during a time when a "chain store" would have been a place that sold chains. We strolled by the local merchants, who were starting to adorn their shops with black ribbon and with whom we exchanged a few words of consolation. There was Trinque's Drugstore, where you could sit and enjoy a strawberry Coke; Crovo's Grocery, where you could buy all you wanted just by saying, "Charge it, Fred"; and Hill's Five-and-Dime, back when you could actually buy something for five or ten cents. It was in Hill's that we found an object for a mere fifteen cents, which has become priceless and has been an inspiration for countless years: a small unfinished boxer made of plaster. Dad promised that together we could paint it to look like Pepper, our beloved Boston terrier.

So father and son sat in the kitchen, working together, with the television on in the background relaying the latest details. While black-and-white images flickered on the television, black and white paint decorated the little dog. Black-and-white images reflected a troubled world; black and white paint reflected a decent one: family, community, and the dedication of parents who care, long before catchy phrases like "quality time" graced our language. Amidst the tragedy, we found reassurance. What our country seemed to be searching for, my father and I found in each other.

A young man does not take such things with him to Boy Scout camp, to the dormitory at college, or to the summer job in Montana. But when he becomes a man, he learns to appreciate things a bit more. One day, I found the dog in a box in my parents' basement. Time had not been particularly kind; the dog had been chipped and broken and glued together several times over the years. Dad, in his wisdom, turned it into something positive.

"Makes it even better," was his surprising remark. "Reminds us that we will get knocked down in life and will get up again. You will too, my son."

So it was, and so it is. We find the strength to go on, braced by loved ones, friends, and community.

Today, when I walk through my hometown with Dad, now in his eighties, signs of that fateful day are gone. Though some of the shops have been torn down, what remain are the things that can never be torn down—memories of love, family, and community that provide comfort when life is difficult. And for me, there remains one more thing—a beat-up little dog on my dresser, reminding me of what is right and decent about our world.

In case of fire, it goes first. ∽

Tea for Three

by Claudia McCormick | *Red Bluff, California*

IT WAS AN UNINSPIRED, limited kind of town with lots of hot sun, and red dirt that got under your fingernails and in your sandwiches. The town was holding on for dear life to a department store and a couple of taverns and coffee shops near the clock tower, just waiting to be discovered by developers.

But long before the developers found Red Bluff, California, I spent a part of my childhood in an old, decaying two-story structure in a shabby section near the railroad tracks in the center of town. It had once been a stately manner house with lush gardens and apple orchards, but it had been divided into apartments decades before our arrival.

The kitchen was my favorite part of the house because it was in one of the sunny corners of the room that my play table and chairs and tea set were kept. It was there that I hosted a series of weekly, or sometimes daily, tea parties for several dolls and a few imaginary friends.

The preparations were elaborate; the miniature cups placed on saucers in just the right position and the blue glazed teapot set in the middle of the table. Paper napkins, which I sometimes adorned with laboriously drawn flowers, were folded and placed at each setting.

Tea parties always required a selection of tasty treats, and I would devote an hour or more to the task, using a few utensils found in the back of the kitchen cupboards: an empty two-pound coffee can, a wooden spoon, and a rusty lid from an old flour canister.

I relied on two proven recipes for my party. One recipe was for a mud pound cake, which also doubled as a meatloaf. The other recipe, which was for cookies, consisted of one adult-size cup of soft, dark red dirt; some water; a handful of gravel or small pebbles; and a flower in full bloom. I would mix the ingredients in the coffee can with the spoon, making sure the rocks were evenly distributed. Then, taking a handful at a time, I molded the mixture into round, plump cookies, garnished each with flower petals, and arranged them on the rusty lid for serving. The recipe served four dolls.

Two of my dolls, Maude Amy and Maggie, were always welcome for tea because they were the only ones who could be propped up on chairs without periodically sliding under the table. The other two, somewhat reluctant guests, a sock doll named Henny and a Raggedy Andy doll, frequently slumped to the floor just as I was pouring the tea. My attempts at rearranging their stuffing by twisting and pummeling never seemed to work.

Before long, both would be permanently assigned to the floor while I carried on an animated conversation with Maude Amy and Maggie. I spoke for the three of us, and I wish I could remember what we talked about because I'm sure it was full of doll wisdom that I could use today.

Many years later, I returned to the area to visit my daughter Kathleen. We sat at her sunny kitchen table in her country home cradling our tea mugs and talking. We watched as a hummingbird fluttered and drank and propelled itself backward in the lush garden below the kitchen window. At the same time, we watched Stevie

Leigh, my three-year-old granddaughter, as she prepared for a tea party.

I watched in delight as she carefully set out the tiny saucers and cups, moving them this way and that until they were in the right position. I watched as she placed the blue glazed teapot in the center of the table.

During a brief lull in our conversation, I noticed the tea party guests being carried to the table. Two dolls, Brenda and Becky, were placed in chairs in front of their teacups. It did not take long before they began the inevitable slow slide off their chairs to the floor. As the scene repeated itself many times during the next quarter hour, I could sense the hostess losing her patience. My heart went out to her. I wanted to tell my granddaughter about organizing successful doll tea parties, but I knew she would learn these secrets on her own, just as I had.

While my daughter and I enjoyed the warmth of her kitchen, refreshed our cups and talked of small-town matters, the tea party progressed beneath us. I noticed Brenda and Becky's legs were sufficiently, if somewhat grotesquely bent, and their arms propped on the table so they were finally immobile in their chairs and hunched over the place settings. The other guest, a Pooh bear, stared blankly ahead from his position under the table.

Stevie Leigh paused for a moment and studied the tea table. Suddenly, she disappeared into the garden and returned moments later with a white daisy. I smiled as she quickly pulled away the petals and arranged them around a plate of red-hued, thimble-size rocks next to the teapot.

The lump in my throat confirmed the fact that Stevie Leigh and I are connected through life and through tea tables, despite the generations that separate us. I think of my granddaughter and the detailed arrangements we have now shared at our tea parties. We have designed, mixed, shaped, created, cajoled, and decorated. We have spoken for those who cannot speak, and dealt with the frustration of guests slipping under the table. In the same wonderful way, we have shared the same treasured childhood memories; a simple home in a small western town, and a series of very successful tea parties. ∽ᱬ

Kentucky Girl

by Leslie J. Wyatt | *Leitchfield, Kentucky*

SHE COULDN'T WAIT TO LEAVE the little Kentucky town of Leitchfield in the central hills of Grayson County. It may have been the county seat and full of up-and-coming plans, even during the time of the Great Depression, but to this seventeen-year-old girl, life in Leitchfield loomed before her like a prison sentence.

In her mind, her ticket out was to leave high school and elope with a local boy. But instead of finding her dream life, she spent the next six years in Leitchfield and adjoining towns, trying to make the marriage work. Finally, at the age of twenty-four, with a young daughter in tow and the country at war, she left a failing marriage and a town full of relatives, and headed for the big city of Louisville where she took a job in the Curtis-Wright aircraft plant.

In some ways her life was exciting, full of independence and dreams, and the small-town life she'd left behind seemed ever so dull in comparison. She never really missed it, especially when she met and fell in love with a handsome draftsman in the design department. Oh, it was hard—incredibly so—when he enlisted and got shipped to the South Pacific, but she kept working, sent him photos of herself and her daughter, and wrote letters wishing he were back home. With no transportation, she rarely got down to Leitchfield to see her family, though they lived only a couple of hours away. But life was wide-open and exciting and full of challenges. Even an afternoon sitting in the porch swing of her parents' house chafed her.

So when her sailor returned home at the end of the war and joined his parents and brothers in the high desert country of Southwest Colorado, it wasn't too difficult to wave goodbye to the lush green hills of Kentucky and board a bus for the West and accept his marriage proposal. At twenty-eight, this Kentucky girl could only look forward.

Forward to Colorado. Big. Open. Dry. Full of piñon pines and sagebrush. Everything was different—new husband, new land, new ways of relating. Her new extended family, so different from her own laughing, sprawling relations, lived together on a homestead carved out of the canyons and dry ground. Life in the big log house wasn't always trouble-free, but she was too busy looking forward to miss the easy acceptance she always found from her own family.

She got her teaching certificate and walked two miles one way, daughter in tow, to teach school in a one-room schoolhouse much like the one from her own childhood. Winter came and snow lay deep and stayed long. Spring arrived at last, then summer, dry and warm, and as year followed year, she came to love Colorado.

There might have been times when she longed for the water, the greenness, the folks back home in Kentucky. But if she missed the things back home she never dwelt too long on them.

So time passed, as time will, and her child grew up, married, and moved just down the road. The early days of grandbabies and Christmas mornings sped by. Then one day in autumn she watched her daughter and family drive off to a new life in Montana, a thousand miles away. Perhaps it was after that, when voices of grandchildren no longer livened the quiet corners of her house and heart, that the Kentucky girl's thoughts turned back to the little town of Leitchfield, so far away. She thought of her own parents, grown old, and to sisters and brothers now middle-aged like herself.

Somewhere in the next few years, like a seed long dormant, a desire began to sprout, send out delicate roots, and finally break through the surface. She wanted to go home. And what was to keep her away, now that daughter and grandchildren had gone?

Fifteen hundred miles—across high desert and into the Kansas plains—her tires rolled. Then plains gave way to the rolling hills of the Ozarks, and wave after wave of memories swept over her. Strange, how time had altered her pictures of home. Had she really thought it a prison? How could that be when it held so many dear people and memories, and she knew every street and landmark for miles around?

Oh, the green, green hills of Kentucky! There across the broad Ohio River they beckoned, and then all at once, she was back—back to the country of her birth and childhood, and how sweet—how incredibly dear it had become in the years since she had walked out the doors of high school for the final time.

There was the little white house with its porch swing. There was Mammaw, flapping her apron and fighting tears, and Pappaw, surrounded by his coon hounds, waving a work-hardened hand.

Siblings and cousins, aunts, uncles—she was related to half the town—greeted her. And after an absence of more than thirty years, it was still as if she had never been gone. How familiar the streets, the country, the way of life. Within weeks, her accent, which had become hardened by the dry western speech, mellowed, reclaiming its soft, southern twang.

Strange, how deeply the familiar things stirred her now— deeply, to her very roots. For it was here, the hills of central Kentucky, that everyone from her parents to her great-great-great-grandparents had called home. And it was here, to this small and suddenly precious place, that the Kentucky girl had at last returned. ᐸᔅ

Legacy in a Soup Pot

by Barbara Davey | *North Arlington, New Jersey*

HAVE YOU EVER NOTICED the busier your life seems to be, the more empty it appears to become? I remember staring at my date book one Monday morning—scores of meetings, deadlines, and projects leered back at me, demanding my attention. An aging baby boomer, I had been climbing the proverbial corporate ladder for over twenty-five years. I had worked hard, earned a coveted corner office, wore designer suits, and frequented the hottest social clubs in the city. However, a nagging emptiness continued to permeate my thoughts and I remember ruminating for the umpteenth time whether any of it really mattered.

Lately, I'd begun remembering my beloved grandmother and the lovely little town I grew up in. The sleepy township of North Arlington, New Jersey, a one-horse type of community, consisted of a post office, a police station, a town hall, a small library, two churches, and a diner where everyone gathered for coffee and conversation each morning. Here, information about the residents of North Arlington was freely exchanged. If someone was in trouble, the community was ready to help with cash, coffee, conversation, or just a shoulder to lean upon.

Looking back, I suppose Grandma was a stereotypical resident, with a sixth-grade education, an abundance of kitchen-table wisdom, and a wonderful sense of humor. Everyone she met said it was appropriate that she had been born on April Fool's Day—she certainly spent her lifetime buoying up everyone's spirits. Every activity with Gram became an event, an occasion to celebrate, a reason to laugh. She loved everything, including nature. She especially always loved birds.

"If I could come back here as something else, it would be a bird—a big red one," she said. When I asked why, she had answered, "Because birds are beautiful. They fly like God's angels."

Years later, I tried to recapture Gram's affinity with nature. One winter, I coaxed my husband into helping me assemble an elaborate birdfeeder outside our kitchen window. For weeks, I'd filled it with gourmet birdseed only to have the wind scatter the seeds. Looking back, I realized I had never seen a bird near the feeder, so I eventually stopped filling it.

But as much as Gram enjoyed her birds, meals were her mainstay—occasions to be planned, savored, and enjoyed. Hot, sit-down breakfasts were mandatory. The preparation of lunch began at 10:30 every morning with homemade soup set to simmering. Dinner plans started at 3:30 P.M. with a call to the local butcher to make a delivery. Gram spent a lifetime meeting the most basic needs of her family.

That evening, as I stopped to pick up yet another take-out meal, my mind traveled back to Gram's kitchen. The old oak kitchen table, with the single pedestal . . . the endless pots of soups, stews, and gravies perpetually simmering on the stovetop . . . the homey tablecloths stained with love from a meal past. *My gosh,* I thought with a start. *I'm forty-seven years old, and I have yet to make a pot of soup or stew from scratch!*

The following day, I rummaged through the attic searching for a certain cardboard box that had been stowed away. Thirty years ago, the box had been given to me when Gram decided to move from the old homestead. I remember the day vividly. Some of the old-time residents still lived there. Many came to say goodbye to Gram, but even as I watched, I sensed that change was under way. I knew that once Gram had moved, I would never return to the old homestead again.

I'd been a teen at the time and only vaguely remember going through my inheritance box. Every granddaughter had received a pocketbook—mine was a jeweled evening bag, circa 1920. I carried it at my college graduation, but never really bothered with the rest of the contents, which remained sealed in that same box, buried somewhere in the attic. Now as I looked, the box wasn't that difficult to locate. The tape was old and gave way easily. Lifting the top, I saw Gram had wrapped some items in old linen napkins—a butter dish, a vase, and at the very bottom, one of her old soup pots. The lid was taped to the pot itself. I pealed back the tape and removed the lid. At the bottom of the pot was a letter, penned in Gram's own hand.

My darling Barbara,

I know you will find this one day many years from now . . . While you are reading this please remember how much I loved you, for I'll be with the angels then, and I won't be able to tell you myself . . .

You were always so headstrong, so quick, so much in a hurry to grow up. I often had wished that I could have kept you a baby forever . . . When you stop running, when it's time for you to slow down, I want you to take out your Gram's old soup pot, and make your house a home. I have enclosed the recipe for your favorite soup, the one I used to make for you when you were my baby.

Remember I love you, and love is forever . . .

Your Gram

I read the note over and over that morning, sobbing that I had not appreciated her enough when I had her. That morning, the disasters of the outside world were put on hold. I had a pot of soup to make, and for once, my priority was clear.

Hours later, a familiar aroma began to waft through the kitchen. It was as if Gram were here again. Not wanting any of my precious memory to escape, I got up to close the kitchen window. At first, I thought I had imagined it, so I blinked. But it was still there. Sitting in the middle of my empty birdfeeder, cocking its head and staring at me, was the most beautiful, brilliant cardinal I had ever seen. ⌒⌒

The Borough of North Arlington, New Jersey

Population: 15,181

Town Facts

First incorporated: 1896

Transportation: Buses travel from the Borough of North Arlington to the Port Authority Bus Terminal in New York City. The closest airport is Newark Liberty International Airport.

Location: North Arlington is located in Bergen County, about ten miles from New York City, northeast of Newark between Kearny and Lyndhurst along State Highway 17 near the Hackensack River.

North Arlington is part of the Bergen-Passaic, New Jersey, metro area. The Passaic River as well as the Belleville and New Jersey turnpikes are less than a mile away.

History: One of the pivotal events in North Arlington history was the discovery of copper ore in 1713, on the property of Arent Schuyler. The Schuyler copper mine financed the development of the entire area for nearly a century, and saw the beginnings of the Industrial Revolution in America.

※ ——————— ※

1715—The mine was shipping roughly 100 tons of copper ore per year.

1743—Unfortunately, drift mining was no longer considered productive, so the facility converted to shaft mining. Worker Malachi Vanderpoel was killed when he fell down a 100-foot shaft sunk sometime around 1735. The shaft became known as the Victoria Shaft, and was reputed to be the first shaft ever sunk in the United States.

1749—The mine is visited by Benjamin Franklin, who writes, in a letter to Jared Eliot on February 13, 1750, that the mine is not being worked because of flooding and that "they [wait] for a fire-engine from England to drain their pits."

1753—The engine arrives and is taken to Victoria Shaft, the mine's deepest shaft.

1755—It takes a year and a half to assemble the engine. Early in 1755, it is set into operation, making this the first time steam power has been employed in the New World. The Victoria Shaft is made deeper as work progresses.

1760—A new brass cylinder for the engine is shipped from London.

1793—The mine remains idle during the Revolution.

1801—The old steam engine is dismantled and sold in pieces.

1876—The purported relic of the original Schuyler steam engine, the four-foot section of cast iron said to have been part of the cylinder, is displayed at the Centennial Exposition in Philadelphia, with a letter from Joseph P. Bradley, Associate Justice of the U.S. Supreme Court, certifying it as part of "The first ever (steam engine) erected on this continent." (Bradley is the grandson-in-law of Josiah Hornblower, who originally created the steam engine.)

1889—The relic is placed in the Smithsonian Institution.

Letting Go

by Loretta Miller Mehl | *Hill Creek, Arkansas*

AFTER THE JAPANESE ATTACKED PEARL HARBOR, young men from Hill Creek, our rural community near Plumerville, Arkansas, raced to sign up for military duty.

At first, no one in our family qualified for military service. My older brother, Hershel, had just celebrated his sixteenth birthday four days before the bombing. By his seventeenth birthday, however, he yearned to join his friends who already served in far-off places.

"But you don't need to be drafted. Farmers are exempt!" My father said, appearing distraught.

Hershel quickly replied. "Only cowards refuse to enlist! All the guys are volunteering!"

"You're too young! Wait till you're older."

"I can't wait!" Hershel declared. "Once I'm drafted they'll put me anyplace they wish. Please, Daddy, I want to join the Navy!"

The argument continued for months, but a parent's signature was required before Hershel could volunteer, and eventually, he wore my father down. A son who was terribly unhappy would accomplish little at home. With deep misgivings, Daddy gave his consent and the two left for the recruiting office.

The officer in charge issued instructions that Hershel leave the following Saturday. He had only four days to finish all the details of civilian life. On the fourth day, Daddy took Hershel to town. Unable to speak of his love, Daddy waited until the last moment, then grabbed Hershel's shoulders and pulled him tightly to his heart. Sending his firstborn off to war must have been an enormous sacrifice.

It seemed like an eternity since the attack on Pearl Harbor had occurred. We listened to all the news reports, prayed for Hershel, and waited eagerly for the postman to bring the precious V-mails. Although the letters were censored, Hershel revealed that he was on the *Bismarck Sea,* an aircraft carrier. He did not write about the war activities. Instead, he wrote about his friends. One was the ship's chaplain, and he and my brother shared similar backgrounds. They talked about Sunday-morning church services and the hymns they sang. The chaplain spoke about his wife and two young children and how eager he was to return home.

Then one day in February 1945, when Hershel had been gone for over two years, Mother and Daddy left to go to town. They stopped by Aunt Altie's house for a list of grocery items to buy for her, and while there, a news flash came over the radio. The *Bismarck Sea* had gone down. The casualties were high and the number of survivors unknown.

At the time, I wondered why my parents were returning so suddenly. Then I caught a glimpse of Mama's face, crumpled by grief.

"What is it?" I asked. "What's happened? Tell me, please!" But Mama could only cry.

Daddy finally said, "Hershel's ship has gone down. We don't know if he is dead or alive."

"Oh, God, no!" I prayed, bargained, petitioned, demanded, pleaded, "Father in Heaven, please let him be alive."

A whole week went by with no message from the war department. The wait was painfully slow, but, finally, we received a telegram one day by rural mail delivery. With trembling fingers, Daddy ripped it open.

Dear Mom and Dad,

I am fine. Be home soon.

Love, Hershel

A world renewed. Joy! Hershel was alive and was coming home!

Much later he told us about that long journey. Strangers attempted to befriend him but he wanted to be alone. He thought continually about the friends he'd lost, especially the chaplain who would never go home to his wife and children. In his nightmares, he relived being in the water, trying to keep afloat, while the Japanese planes continued strafing those who escaped the doomed aircraft carrier. The four hours before rescue seemed an eternity.

He came on the bus from the nearest town, getting off at the end of our country road. The whole neighborhood had been watching for him. Noah and Lee Cooper spotted him first. As he passed their house, they came out and walked with him. At the next house, the Robinson family joined the group, asking Hershel if he was all right.

"Yes, I'm fine," he murmured, "but most of my friends on the flight deck were killed."

"What happened to your ship?" they asked.

"We suffered two direct hits. Kamikaze planes."

Noah gently touched Hershel's arm. "I'm sorry, Hersh. I'm so terribly sorry."

Hershel turned to him with anguish in his eyes. "Why so many of my friends and not me?"

When Aunt Altie and Uncle Will saw him, they came running out to the road. Aunt Altie hugged him fiercely to her ample bosom while tears slid slowly down her wrinkled cheeks. "Oh, thank the Lord, you're safe!" she whispered.

The group now walked in silence. They passed the big tree in front of Uncle Joe's house, the graveyard where his grandparents were buried, and then as they topped the small knoll, Hershel could see the farmhouse. The neighbors continued to march alongside, supporting him, loving him.

Hershel hurried now. He was almost home—a safe place from the tragedies of war. He came through the center hallway quickly and called, "Mom, Dad, anybody here?"

"He's home!" I cried. "He's home!" I left my job of cracking hickory nuts and ran to him. Mama, shaking with emotion, flung her arms around her firstborn, tears flowing down her face. We all reached out to touch him, weeping with joy.

Daddy, the strong farmer who seldom showed emotion, cried openly. "He came home," he said, as if he still couldn't believe it. "He really came home!" ᘖ

The Heart of the River

by Paul L. Ziemer as told to Lori Z. Scott | *Indian River, Michigan*

I GREW UP WITH INDIAN RIVER, and it grew up with me.

I remember traveling "up north" as a child to stay at this small tourist town in Michigan. Excitement always seized my sisters and me when we finally smelled the telltale pine trees and spotted lines of pearly white birch, bright against the emerald wood of our home away from home.

While water boxes cooled by artesian well water kept our food cold, a pot-bellied stove kept our cabin warm. Often, when the nip of evening settled on the town, we snuggled in the stove's cozy glow. Fed by wood, the stove not only sizzled and popped in a satisfying way, but also released a pleasant smoky odor.

Days spent picking blueberries in the woods, inventing new games to play, or helping with chores made this town seem magical. However, the best part of Indian River was fishing with my dad.

My sisters had little patience with the rod, so, without waking them, the two of us snuck out to our favorite spot, the Walleye Hole. The hushed sounds of the lake waking up lent an almost reverent quiet to that solitary time. Though we didn't talk much, an intimate bond formed between us, something intangible and precious.

Sometimes boats with local fishermen bobbed nearby hoping to "catch a rainbow," which meant hooking the prize of the lake, the elusive rainbow trout. After the sun rose, I listened to their friendly banter and luxuriated in our common mission.

Time passed, I matured, and life changed. A new interstate replaced the gravel roads, providing easier access to the town. Furnaces and refrigerators accommodated cabins. My siblings and I brought our spouses and boisterous children, swelling our ranks to twenty. A new curiosity was erected, The Cross in the Woods Shrine.

Yet, despite the variations, the important things about Indian River, like its comfortable sense of belonging and daily routines, remained. The fishermen still owned daybreak. My old dependable outboard motor still came to life with a *vroom*, the hazy smell of burning gas, and a *putt-putt-putt*. Wearing my lucky straw hat with a faded blue swordfish and a piece of netting sewed to the top, I habitually maneuvered our rowboat to the Walleye Hole. My children came along, dressed in cutoff jeans, T-shirts, and bright orange lifejackets.

Like my father had done with me, I taught my kids how to cast a line without getting tangled in the weeds (and other people). Time replayed itself when their thin lines flickered across the water like spider draglines, and bait hit with a *plink* before disappearing beneath the surface.

On clear days, I took the kids into the heart of the lake where the wind blew in a light stream. Sometimes I opened the throttle and we'd slap over the waves like a flat-bellied seal while the boat threw a playful spray of water into our faces.

Each year, I vowed not to shave until I caught a rainbow trout. This provided a good excuse to grow a beard. If my wife ever complained about my shadowy scruff, I'd simply exclaim, "Can't shave. Haven't caught my rainbow!"

In the evening, we men cleaned and gutted the day's catch of walleye and bass. The women fried it in crispy batter seasoned with lemon, creating the best fish I've ever eaten. The youngsters, finding a lull in activity, played kick-the-can.

When the aroma of sizzling fish permeated the cabin and wafted out the doors, kids raced pell-mell to the kitchen, arriving barefoot and flushed. Chatter ended as each person grabbed a hand and bowed their head. Together, in the sudden stillness, we prayed. Then with a burst of activity and the clatter of dishes, all jockeyed for a seat at the table. A mixed bag of conversation and uproarious laughter bubbled out from the main dining area while others babbled on the screened porch.

We paid the kids five cents for every bone they found, a ploy to keep them from gobbling their food too fast and choking. They hunted for bones like they would a treasure, knowing that five stray bones earned a quarter, enough to buy a comic book.

As the sun melted over the water, we played endless rounds of card games. Outside, crickets serenaded us with gentle songs and fireflies winked against the velvet sky.

Each night when fatigue finally claimed me, I climbed into bed with a smile on my lips. I felt at peace there, sleeping with those who loved me most in the world nestled close by. Just as I had as a child, I dreamed about the morrow and the flashing silver of a leaping trout catching dawn's first rays.

Now, twenty-five years later, I returned to Indian River. But while the thrill of anticipation coursed through my sixty-five-year-old body, I wasn't prepared for the way the town felt. It seemed so familiar and so foreign at the same time.

Gulls still drifted overhead, crying a native welcome. Waves lapped the shoreline as they had in summers past. A sappy aroma yet lingered in the air, people still sunned in the warm cinnamon-and-sugar sand, and boats continued to dance across Burt Lake.

But other changes had overtaken the town. The storefronts I knew so well now sagged like tired hounds, yet the beach seemed perkier, with its shiny new playground equipment. Even so, the dog-eared pages of memory colored the vision before me. In a wistful sort of way, like the kiss of a whispering wind on bare skin, my eyes saw one thing but my heart saw something else.

Indian River, like me, had aged, but it still possessed an enchantment and intimacy whose deep-seated value was measured by the laugh lines on my face. Somehow, it had developed a different, richer kind of beauty. Part of that beauty abides in perception.

I came back to Indian River only to find that I had never really left it behind. I had taken it with me. ᧿

Shopping Spree

by Linda Kaullen Perkins | *Sedalia, Missouri*

IT SEEMED STRANGE LEAVING COLLEGE and coming back home to Sedalia, Missouri, to teach where I had gone to grade school. But strange or not, I would begin student teaching in two weeks.

As I walked down the halls of Jefferson School, I stopped at the first-grade classroom. It hadn't changed much. I could still remember my first-grade teacher, Mrs. Riddle, handing me a dime and saying, "Linda, run down to Walter's Market and get me a Coca-Cola, dear. And, hurry now."

Walter's Market! For a child, there was no more glorious place than Walter's Market. I had run down to Walter's Market many times in the years growing up, but one particular time stood out in my mind. It was the time I decided to become a big spender.

"Remember, get lettuce, not cabbage," Mama had called through the screen door.

I nodded and started down the sidewalk, fingering the ten-dollar bill and grocery list in my pocket. Mr. Lane, sitting on his front porch, touched his hat as if I was a lady instead of an eight-year-old kid.

By the time I reached Walter's Market, the hot Missouri sun had done a number on me and sweat trickled down my forehead. I didn't mind. I knew the white cinder-block building would be cool. I smiled as I pulled the brass handle. The sign on the glass door read, WELCOME TO SEDALIA, MISSOURI. COOL INSIDE. And it was cool. It felt as good inside Walter's Market as it did in Marvel Cave down at Silver Dollar City.

Inside, my friend Barbara had just dropped a coin into the pop machine. Raising the lid on the chest-type cooler, she slid a glass bottle along the rack. With a loud clank, the machine released an ice-cold bottle of Coke. Helen, half owner of the market, never said a word, just produced a cloth and wiped the counter when Barbara set down the wet bottle and pulled a dime from her pocket.

"Oh. Sorry, Helen," Barbara apologized. "Would you give me a bag of peanuts, please?"

Helen smiled, turned around, and found the peanuts with a quick glance. She could probably have found Tootsie Rolls, Val-o-milks, or Chiclets with her eyes closed.

I walked away as Barbara dumped the bag of peanuts into her Coke and slurped and chomped on the fizzy drink. In the farthest of the three main aisles, I stopped at the cooler along the wall, comparing lettuce and cabbage. I was all the way back to the cash register, choosing a loaf of bread, before I realized I'd forgotten the lunchmeat and had to retrace my steps to the back of the store where Dorsey, the other half owner, leaned on his elbows and peered down at me from behind the white refrigeration unit. Beneath his sideways paper hat, he pushed at his ever-sliding glasses.

"What can I do for you today, kiddo?"

"I need half a pound of baloney." I pointed, then rested my finger on the glass.

He reached past the cheese, between the liverwurst and pickle loaf. Flipping on the whining slicer, he fed in the huge stick of meat, resting the end against his once-white apron. With a flourish, he ripped a square of white paper off a roll, laid it on the scale, and stacked the slices.

At the cash register, I handed Helen the ten-dollar bill. It seemed a shame to lug home the tremendous amount of change, so that particular day, I decided to buy presents. Mama got red finger-nail polish. Daddy got orange slices and bacon rinds. I bought cheese curls, soda pop, and ice cream for myself.

I started out of the store as Barbara took the last swig of Coke. "I only have three pennies left," I said aloud, more to myself than anyone.

"You might as well put those in the gumball machine," Barbara said, setting her Coke bottle in the wooden case. "Maybe you'll get a speckled ball and win some free candy." But after three twists of the gumball machine, I stuffed my unlucky gum into my mouth and grabbed the bulging sack of groceries. It wasn't until that blast of hot air hit me that my conscience kicked in and I wondered what Mama would say about my shopping spree.

Unfortunately, she had plenty to say. With a cross look and her finger pointing in my face, she practically yelled, "Your daddy works hard for that money. How could you waste it so foolishly?" All I could think to mumble was that it was Barbara's fault. "Why?" she demanded, with an expression that said she wasn't buying my story.

"Because Barbara said I should put the three pennies into the gumball machine." I added lamely, "Maybe I would get a speckled ball." Mama's wilting look was worse than a spanking.

I ducked out of the first-grade classroom and continued down the hall, chuckling as I recalled my errand-running days and the humiliation I felt each time Mama sent me to the store after that. "I need you to run down to Walter's Market," she would say pleas-antly; then with her eyebrows raised for emphasis, she always added, "And, *don't* buy anything extra." ॐ

Swimming for St. Peter

by Nan B. Clark | *Gloucester, Massachusetts*

FOR GENERATIONS, GLOUCESTER FISHERMEN dressed as pirates, mermaids, and ballerinas have skidded their way to glory on a slippery wooden pole suspended over the harbor, screaming, "Viva San Pedro!" as they plunged into the sea.

Even today girls don't walk the plank. But once upon a time, I did.

The forty-five-foot telephone pole extends year-round from a wooden platform 200 feet off Pavilion Beach. Every June during the festival honoring St. Peter, patron saint of fishermen, the pole is plastered with giant chunks of gear grease and a red flag is stuck upright into its tip, attracting dozens of young men who compete to snatch it from its perch and become the town hero.

Gloucester takes up most of tiny Cape Ann on the northern coast of Massachusetts. Jutting out into the Atlantic like a big fishhook itself, the cape has attracted European fishermen for four centuries. When my grandparents came from Portugal in 1893 they must have felt right at home, even if the brutal winters sometimes freeze the harbor into jagged blue-white chunks, because in the summer it's pure Mediterranean.

Brightly painted three- and four-story houses with their tiers of porches groaning with terracotta pots of geraniums and marigolds overlook the harbor where both pleasure and fishing boats sway with the tide. The voice of the Old Country still calls out from Our Lady of Good Voyage Church with her melodious chimes made of bells cast from the same foundry as the Liberty Bell. The Portuguese community has always clustered around this beautiful structure, feeling the protection of the heavens in the form of a huge, painted statue of the Virgin Mary gazing out to sea from the rooftop with the model of a schooner tucked in her arms.

During the early decades of the twentieth century, Italian Catholics swelled the fishing fleet. The St. Peter's Fiesta gained in popularity as both a religious event and a secular spectacle of glorious color. In late June, the streets glitter with arcs of lights shaped into miraculous blossoms leading to a temporary altar where the statue of the saint views both the blessing of the fleet and the carnival atmosphere of the harbor games.

Nat Misuraca became the first fisherman to walk the greasy pole for the glory of God and Gloucester back in 1931, five years before I was born. From 1940 to 1945, nobody walked that smeared, black plank thanks to the war. But when the boys came home, they slipped back into the games of their youth, hoisting the winner onto their shoulders and carrying him up Pavilion Beach to the applause of family and friends.

I fulfilled my dream to walk the greasy pole the summer I turned fifteen. The full moon of August glowed like a beacon as I picked my way over the broken mussel shells and speckled pebbles dotting the cool sand. It was high tide. I slipped into the water knowing that in a few strokes I'd be over my head. Barely lifting my face from the water, I zeroed in on the black silhouette of the platform.

After I pulled myself up the gray wood ladder, I just stood for a moment, shivering in fear and excitement, before stepping onto the pole. Of course, there was no red flag at the tip, and the huge chunks of grease were missing, too, but the wood was still disgustingly slippery as my bare toes tried to curl around it.

I edged my way out six inches, perhaps, and then another six. I waved my arms as my feet danced a perilous pirouette, my eyes trying not to focus on the black water below. Farther out in the harbor, past Ten Pound Island, I could see the red and green twinkle of port and starboard lights as late-coming vessels slipped into port, and the synchronized flash of the Eastern Point lighthouse on the horizon.

For a second, I held a great gulp of fresh air deep in my lungs, pungent with fish and salt odors so familiar they would always seem like the only true air to me. Then, just before I lost my balance completely, I plunged off the side of the pole, whispering, "Viva San Pedro!"

After high school, I married a navy man and we lived all over the world. Whenever we settled down in a port, I'd think of the black, rippling water surrounding the greasy pole, and how, after the blessing of the fleet, bright petals would float on the surface like miniature boats.

In time, we came back to the states and eventually to Gloucester, where the greasy pole still rose from the harbor like a kid's construction of weathered Popsicle sticks. Neither time, nor tide, nor the affairs of men had destroyed this special feature of my hometown. In fact, the St. Peter's Fiesta was bigger and better than ever, attracting television and movie crews and magazine writers who interviewed anybody dressed in a tutu or eye patch.

One night when the tide was high, I swam out to the platform with my husband at my side. "Think you could capture the flag?" I asked him.

He squinted up. "Maybe if somebody lowered me from a plane."

I laughed and started back toward shore, reveling in the confirmation that the greasy pole was just as awesome as I had remembered it to be, and that St. Peter was still watching out for his own. ᕲ

Song at Sunrise

by Leigh Platt Rogers | *Tusayan, Arizona*

DUE TO MY FATHER'S PROFESSION as a CIA operative, I spent the majority of my childhood abroad. From the age of five, until I turned seventeen, I was whisked from country to country, moving every several years. Although I was able to speak three languages and was culturally educated, I lacked roots—that sense of "belonging" somewhere. As a young girl growing up in a most un-American way, I had no concept of what it meant to be an American.

After my family and I returned to the United States, I felt restless and disconnected. My reintroduction to the American culture had been difficult and I never felt like I fit in. When my aunt invited me to come and stay with her in California, I took advantage of the opportunity and quickly made preparations for the drive across the country. Perhaps a change was what I needed.

Most of the trip was uneventful. I endured the monotony of highway scenery by listening to the radio and taking short breaks. When I reached Arizona, I decided to head for Tusayan—a small town located outside the legendary Grand Canyon National Park.

I arrived at dusk and looked for a motel for the night. I decided that if I felt like it in the morning, I'd take a quick trip to see the canyon and then be on my way.

After finding a motel, I went by a small diner for a bite to eat. As soon as I walked in, it was obvious to me the place was frequented by locals. I was the recipient of many curious looks as I found a table and sat down. A large waitress bustled over and gave me a menu. There was not much to choose from. I decided on something simple: a cheeseburger with fries. I was in the middle of my dinner when an elderly couple stopped by my table on their way out and asked where I was from. Wiping a dot of mustard from the side of my mouth while trying to swallow the huge bite I had just taken, I managed to say, "Northern Virginia."

"Oh." They both nodded.

"And where are you headed?" the woman asked.

"California." I paused, feeling like I had to explain myself. "My aunt lives there."

"Ahhhh . . ." They nodded. "So, have you been to the canyon?"

"No, not yet," I replied. "Maybe tomorrow if I have time."

Genuine alarm crossed both faces. "Oh, child," said the woman, "you simply *must* go and see the Old Man. You must!"

The gentleman beside her nodded vehemently. "Yes," he said. "Go to the vista first thing tomorrow. Get there for the sunrise."

"Ooooooh, yes child!" The woman agreed, hands waving. "Go and see the sunrise! It's magnificent!"

I hesitated, glancing back and forth between the animated, friendly faces, and then said, "Well, okay. I guess that sounds like a good idea. Thanks—thanks a lot."

The gentleman put his arm around his companion and they both beamed with obvious pleasure. "Good," he said. "We guarantee you won't regret it!"

Strangely enough, as I watched them leave, I felt happy that they appeared so delighted. I decided then and there that I would follow through and go see the sun rise over the "Old Man."

After a fairly good night's sleep, I got up very early. The drive to the canyon was peaceful—the darkness before the dawn was soothing and cool. When I arrived at the vista point, there was already a small group of visitors who apparently had the same idea that I did. It felt awkward standing shoulder-to-shoulder with strangers, but I was anxious to get a good spot to see the sunrise.

We were all very quiet standing there in the dark, waiting. There were a few whispers here and there, but as soon as the faint glow of the rising sun could be seen, no one uttered a sound. I watched, fascinated as the sky began to slowly change from shades of black and dark blue to hues of red and orange. Directly below us, the walls of the canyon began to glow in faint colors of gold and yellow. Like a canvas being painted right before our eyes, the hills began to take shape—shadows shifting as the sun's rays grew.

Suddenly, from behind, I heard a *click* followed by light strains of music. My arms broke out in goose bumps as I heard the familiar sound of our national anthem fill the air. There was a slight stir among us, but no one turned. Instead, with eyes straight ahead, drinking in the glory of the rising sun, one by one hands rose to cover hearts and the singing began.

As our voices filled the air and echoed into the magnificent canyon below, I felt a shift in my heart with the realization that it was to this country that I belonged. It was as though my heritage revealed itself to me through the breathtaking beauty of the moment—the incredible sunrise over the glorious canyon and the united spirit of the group around me.

After our voices faded, we turned to one another—no longer feeling like strangers—and there was not a dry eye to be seen. Smiling through our tears, we laughed, a collective sound of joy, shook hands, and hugged. Enlightened with my newfound spirit, I continued my drive to California. Because of valuable advice received from two thoughtful folks, I realized, something incredibly important had happened to me: I now knew exactly who I was and where I belonged.

I was finally home. ᴄᴑ

Grandma's Cookie Jar

by Bob Davis | *Rochester Colony, Michigan*

I GREW UP IN MY GRANDPARENTS' HOME in the heart of mid-Michigan, in the '50s. We lived in what was called Rochester Colony. It was part of Duplain Township. Or maybe Duplain Township was part of Rochester Colony—I never could get that straight. All I'm sure about is that we weren't big enough to be considered a town or even a village. We were a rural community.

We had a one-room school for grades K through seven, two churches, a big community park, and a small country store that seemed to change hands every couple of years. It finally closed permanently when I was about twelve.

There were only a couple of dozen homes in the central part of the Colony. The surrounding area consisted of farms. When you put it all together, we had a hundred or so families. People didn't lock their doors, kids could walk the roads without worry, and everyone knew most everyone else. Growing up, it seemed to me everyone knew my grandparents, Harry and Maybelle Beery. And despite the fact the house had no indoor plumbing or running water, no central heat, and no air conditioning, I grew up feeling I was the luckiest kid in the world, or at least a lot luckier than my cousins who lived in town.

You see, I got to live with Grandma and Grandpa. That meant I got to eat Grandma's outstanding cooking every day, and I got to go hunting and fishing with Grandpa on a regular basis. Oh, sure, there were chores that always had to be done, but that was nothing. Especially in light of the fact that I got something every day that my cousins got only when they came to visit. I got access to Grandma's cookie jar.

Grandma's cookie jar was a large, white ceramic owl. It sat in the kitchen just inside the back door on an old wooden flour bin. And it was always filled with the greatest cookies. You never really knew what you'd find when you lifted that owl's head, but you could be sure it would taste great. There were oatmeal cookies, and peanut butter cookies, and oatmeal peanut butter combined. There were ladyfinger, gingerbread, lemon drop, and pumpkin cookies. During the holidays there were Grandma's famous sugar cookies, always appropriately colored with frosting or sugar sprinkles. But my personal favorite, of all the cookies Grandma made, was her chocolate chip with hickory nut.

Grandpa and I gathered those hickory nuts in the nearby woods. I spent many a winter's night in the living room, flatiron on my lap and hammer in my hand, cracking and shelling hickory nuts for Grandma to use in her cookies and other baking.

Years later, after I'd joined the Air Force and moved away, Grandma sent me a bit of home every Christmas. Usually, it was a jar each of her grape jelly, strawberry preserves, and raspberry jam. Some years there was also a loaf of banana nut bread or one of her fruitcakes. And she always sent a big bag of cookies. I never had the heart to tell her the cookies usually arrived crushed. I didn't want to because even the cookie crumbs were a slice of home.

I ended up making the Air Force a career. As a result, we seldom made it home to Michigan. Since my wife is also from Michigan, when we did make it home, we were always pressed for time to try and see everyone. I hadn't realized how much I'd talked about Grandma's cookie jar and her homemade cookies in the stories I told my children, until one particular homecoming in 1985.

My family and I were on our way from England to Texas. We stopped in to see Grandma and Grandpa. Not having been home in three years, we had a lot to catch up on in a very short period. We grown-ups were in the living room, where my grandmother was filling me in on all the changes in the neighborhood, when our oldest daughter, Kimberly, came in from the back of the house. She had her hands clasped in front of her as if she were holding something precious. She sidled up alongside of me and tried to get my attention without interrupting. Finally, I looked at her and asked what she wanted.

Kim opened her hands ever so carefully and held something up for me to see. "Look," she said, "Grandma Beery makes cookies that look just like Oreos."

Grandma overheard her and gave a hearty laugh. "I see you found the owl," she said. "That was always your father's favorite place, too. I don't bake like I did when your father lived here, so I get some store-bought cookies for the owl for when the neighborhood kids stop by. I keep my homemade cookies in a special place."

With that, Grandma turned and led the way to her china bureau. On it was the English Cottage tea set my wife and I had sent her for Christmas the first year we were in England. There along with the teapot, sugar bowl and creamer, and cups and saucers, sat the English Cottage cookie jar. Grandma pulled it down and lifted the lid so Kim could reach inside.

There they were: Grandma's homemade chocolate-chip-with-hickory-nut cookies. Grandma won my daughter's heart that day, and also proved once again, "There's no place like home." ᧬

The Great Potato Patch

by Jean Davidson | *Rupert, Idaho*

As I near Rupert, Idaho, my childhood stomping grounds, I turn off the interstate and head down the dusty dirt road. It's late September and the farm fields are bustling with harvesters. When I drive into the yard, Mom is waiting there, her welcoming smile making me feel like her little girl again.

"They are harvesting the spuds," she says. "Want to watch?" Of course, I do; it's one of the things that tells me autumn has arrived. Together we tramp down to the fields where the harvesters are at work and large trucks are lined up, waiting to be loaded with the beautiful Idaho potatoes. As I watch, my mind carries me back in time and the storytelling begins.

"It's October 1955. We arrive before daylight, so early frost still clings to the potato vines. We rub our gloved hands together to keep circulation going. By sunup, our picking belts are loosely cinched around our waists, weighted down by hooks holding up a half-dozen empty burlap sacks. We shuffle our frost-numbed feet back and forth, waiting as the mechanical harvester belches to life. Moving slowly up one row then down another, it unearths the firm, crisp

Idaho russets from their earthen beds and spreads them evenly atop the ground.

"That's when the older women arrive. The potato-picking mamas of Minidoka County. They stand there, tall and poised, waiting for the go-ahead nod from the harvester's driver before each claims a row by hiking up her picking harness and boldly straddling the chosen row. Then, hunching low and mean over the newly dug spuds, they start.

"'A hundred!' one challenges. A hundred filled bags by day's end. Before the rest of us can finish fussing with our belts, one of the pros already has a sack filled.

"'One,' she yells.

"My friends and I gape in awesome wonder. We haven't even started yet! We hurriedly straddle our selected row, position the burlap bags that will drag between our legs, and start picking. Hunkered low, our fingers snatch up every spud, pitching them under our legs into the trailing gunny sacks.

"It isn't long, however, before the bags get heavy. My pace slows. My arms ache, my muscles cramp, and my back demands I stand upright. But my brain is locked on the challenge. A hundred bags by quitting time.

"'Impossible!'" I mutter.

"I finally surrender and straighten up to ease my back muscles. I wrestle the sack from between my legs and pull it into an upright position. I feel like cheering. My first bag is full! Then I shake it down, and my heart sinks to my knees. The bag isn't even half full yet. Humiliated, I resume picking.

"When finally the bag truly is full, I groan and lug it to the side of the row where the loaders will see it. They will toss it onto the tractor-drawn wagon to be hauled with the other sacks to the spud cellar for storage until time for market. At this moment, however,

I could care less where those spuds are headed. All I can think of is my body screaming at me to stop this foolishness.

"I look around for my friends. They look as bad as I feel. If it weren't for the money, I'd be out of here! But, it is for the money. Ten cents a sack is a lot to a poor country girl. And we desperately want to earn enough to buy ourselves some boy-girl jeans. They sell for $5 a pair at J.C. Penney's. Maybe we can earn enough for black-and-white saddle oxfords, too.

"Thinking of the jeans motivates me back to picking. The hours creep by. Five sacks . . . ten . . . fifteen. My body is numb. Someone calls out 'fifty' and my admiration for her skyrockets. Pure willpower drives me on even as my fogged brain keeps asking why we thought being young, healthy teenagers would automatically make us good potato pickers. A friend whispers it is nearly lunchtime. A beacon in this torturous ordeal!

"Promptly at noon the picking stops. The pros drop their belts, straighten up and stretch, then shake down sacks of spuds to sit on while they eat lunch. They cluster together, laughing and eating and flirting with the cute loader boys who join them. It is all I can do just to unhook my harness and let it drop. I plop down onto the nearest filled potato sack and wait for my friends. We wolf down the wax-paper-wrapped sandwiches brought from home, then shuffle over to the water barrels to quench our thirst. By now the midday sun is blazing hot.

"We revise our goals. Fifty sacks, not a hundred. We're too young for this type of work, right? Fifty will at least buy us new jeans. One friend groans that, jeans or not, she is quitting. We laugh. We all feel like quitting.

"'You'll never reach a hundred if you quit,' a voice behind us says.

"In synchronized motion, we look up to see one of the pros. She is an older woman, maybe nineteen.

"'You can keep going or you can quit. Your choice,' she says. Then she nods toward her friends. 'We won't all make a hundred today, but it won't be because we didn't try. I dare you to keep up.' She grins, winking as she steps past us.

"Her dad must own these fields," I mutter. Everyone bursts into giggles. Nevertheless, when lunchtime ends, we step back into our harnesses and resume picking. She made her point.

"My friends and I never reached the hundred-sack mark, but we kept trying. Eventually, automated machinery displaced us all, but the lesson remains. To get to the row's end, you set the pace and keep on picking. Some days will be hundred-sack days, others will be fifties. So it is with life."

Mother beams at me. She loves to hear the stories of my youth, and is glad I'm home. So am I. ⎘

The Town of Rupert, Idaho

Population: 5,645

History: The Naming of a Town

In the beginning, Rupert was known as Wellfirst. The name seemed appropriate at the time because the town had the only well within miles and people traveled long distances to get their supply of water. Today, the town well, located in the middle of Historic Square Park, is a fountain. The first store, Shilling Store, owned by W. N. Shilling, was not much more than a tarpaper shack in the railroad right-of-way, but it was here that settlers obtained their mail. Then, in 1904, John Henry Rupert, the railroad employee in charge of delivering the mail, had his last name put on his mailbag, and everyone began calling Wellfirst by a new name.

Fun Times: Christmas in Rupert

Rupert received its official Christmas City, USA, title in November 1987. As is tradition in Rupert, Christmas decorations are hung throughout town, and on the Friday following Thanksgiving, Santa makes his much anticipated entrance and lights up Rupert Square. As you are enjoying the Christmas environment, you can have chili, cinnamon rolls, hot chocolate, and coffee. After the Christmas lights in the square are lit, you can sit back and enjoy a grand show of fireworks. Decorations are paid for from the proceeds of the annual Christmas in July breakfast, held at the end of June to kick off the Fourth of July celebration, which includes such fun events as a local parade, a Dutch-oven cook-off, a rodeo, fireworks, a patriotic show, a carnival, many food vendors, and several horse races.

Town Facts

First incorporated: Rupert became incorporated on April 12, 1906.

Transportation: Railroad and auto

Location: Rupert is in south-central Idaho, near Burley and Heyburn, just off I-84. As the crow flies, the distance from Rupert to Washington, D.C., is 2,028 miles, and the distance to the Idaho state capital is 151 miles.

Former name: Wellfirst

Places of note: Rupert is surrounded by beautiful country, including the peaceful Snake River and Lake Walcott, where local historians claim some of the best big game hunting and fishing can be found. In the city, Historic Square Park, found in the center of Rupert, is breathtaking, with a gazebo and arbors, trees, two carved bears, and a fountain. The park is a must-see in the evening when illumination from the old-fashioned lampposts adds a mystical quality to an already beautiful park. Additional area parks include a skateboard park and bike path.

City bird: Ring-necked pheasant

Historic facts:

The first finger steaks originated at the town's Drift Inn.

In 1913, Washington School for seventh through twelfth grade was the first school in the world to have all-electric heat.

Famous Folks

News anchor Lou Dobbs

Actor Bill Fagerbakke

Titanic survivor Anna Donaldson Dunn

When a Second Takes Forever

by Michele Starkey | *Newburgh, New York*

THERE ARE MOMENTS IN OUR LIVES when time seems to fly past, and then there are times when a second seems to take forever. Ask anyone who is stuck in traffic just how long it takes for the seconds to slip past, or try to tell a child to be still while you wait in a long line at the supermarket. Seconds tick by slowly when you stand in the rain waiting for the bus without an umbrella. We all could cite different instances when time stood still for us. For my mother it was the endless emptiness of the time spent waiting for my father to return home from work in 1945.

Father had served as a Navy corpsman during the war and was barely able to support his family as he readjusted to civilian life after his discharge. Work was scarce in the small town of Newburgh, in upstate New York, where my parents lived, and Dad often traveled with my uncle to New Jersey to make extra money.

Prior to the war, Newburgh had been a booming metropolis. Folks from New York City often traveled up the Hudson River by ferryboat just to shop in the downtown waterfront stores. Newburgh's vaudeville theater on Broadway headlined upcoming young stars such as Frank Sinatra and Mary Martin. But the economy changed drastically after the war and most young men were left to commute out of the area for work.

My uncle's 1935 Ford was barely running and yet the two of them climbed onboard to make the five-hour trek across the Jersey border. If they had an extra nickel or two, they stopped and shared a soda along the way. Rarely did they splurge on candy or sweets. They'd rather pocket the change and continue on their way . . . except for one day in the heat of the summer when the old Ford got a flat tire, and then another, and another. The usual five-hour commute turned into ten hours, and the ride home seemed endless as they stopped every fifty miles or so to patch a tire.

At home, my mother was worried sick about the fellas. Worry was no stranger to Mom. She'd waited and worried for four years for Dad to come home from the war. Now she suddenly returned to pacing the floor and watching the clock again.

Only in 1945 would it even be conceivable to patch a flat tire some ten times and continue on the journey. Nowadays, automobile clubs and gas stations make it possible to call for roadside assistance, but at the end of the war times were tough and rubber was hard to come by. Left with nothing but some patch and a lot of sweat, the two men continued the trek home after working all day.

My mother was in tears when the old Ford finally pulled up to the house. The men were covered with road grime, their faces blackened from the day's events. She bolted from the house and into the arms of the man she loved. As he wrapped his strong arms around her, he whispered in her ear, "You don't know how happy I am that we made it home!"

Almost sixty years have passed since that day and my father still laughs as he tells the story about the long ride home. Sometimes getting home is the most important thing that you can ever do—even when it seems that each second takes forever. ೮

The Rag Man

by Lauretta Pauline as told to Michele Wallace Campanelli |
Bellingham, Massachusetts

BELLINGHAM, MASSACHUSETTS, USED TO BE a quiet farming community. But as my husband and I parked our vehicle and looked around at the changes time had brought, I realized Lake Street was much different than it had been sixty years ago. No longer were there acres of corn, peppers, and tomatoes as far as the eye could see, and the street, which had been made of pebbles, now lay paved and well lighted. A dozen new homes dotted the area where cows, chickens, and pigs formerly roamed. But in the center of the block stood my two-story, wood-framed, white farmhouse, now nearly 350 years old. Nothing else had remained the same, except that beautiful hand-hewn home.

As I gazed at the house I couldn't help but notice the difference between the SUV that was parked in front of my old house and the vehicle that used to be parked there—my first Ford.

My mine raced as I remembered my sixteenth birthday and the Model T my father bought me for $25—a bargain in those days. It was an amazing machine: shiny black, with a running board along the sides, two doors, giant head lights, big steering wheel, and a shift stick planted firmly on the floor. Driving that incredible motor car was quite an accomplishment. I was the first in my family to own a vehicle in Bellingham, and the only member to have a driver's license.

With ample experience running a tractor on the farm, I prided myself on being a safe driver on the roads as well. I kept both eyes straight ahead as I streaked down Park Avenue at a daredevil twenty-five miles an hour.

One morning I left home early and ventured into Winsocket to go to the market. There on the side of Lake Street stood a police officer. Before I could even wave hello, he raised his arm and shouted, "Stop! Stop!"

Reaching down, I pulled the clutch and the car rolled to a screeching stop. With wide eyes and a pounding heart, I wondered what I could have done to upset him.

"Good morning, Lauretta," he said.

I smiled as I tried to control my fidgeting. "Did I do something wrong, Officer?"

"Frank," he said. Then he raised his blue hat and I saw how handsome he was. He was about my age, tall and thin, with dark eyes that matched the color of his uniform. A big badge in the shape of a star decorated his strong chest.

"Since this is my lunch break, I'm going to let this go with a warning," he said, "But remember the law. I could have given you a two-dollar ticket. You must give way to horses, pull over to the side, and let them pass."

Just then, a voice echoed down the street. "Rags! Rags! Anyone got rags today?" I turned in time to see an elderly, scruffy-faced man lead a huge, red horse through the mist. The long cart the horse pulled was piled with cloths of all different colors and textures, both dirty and clean.

"I'm sorry, Officer, I didn't see him," I explained.

"You need to be more careful. Horses still aren't used to these motor cars and they can get easily spooked." As he talked, the officer unwrapped a dish towel from around his sandwich and tossed the towel on top of the pile. "There you go, Rag Man."

"Thank you," the Rag Man said, then reached in the back of his cart and quickly tossed the officer a big red apple.

"No bananas today?" the policeman asked, catching the fruit in midair.

"Tomorrow," said the Rag Man with a wrinkly smile as he tipped his hat and plodded on to the next house, his voice ringing in the morning air.

I turned to the officer with a questioning look. "Why is he doing that?"

Now it was the officer's turn to look puzzled. "Don't you know?" He took a quick bite of the fruit, chewing as he explained. "The Rag Man comes down this road every week. He takes the rags people give him to the mill. They crush the material, make new yarn, and then rework it into material for clothes or quilts. For making a donation, the Rag Man gives you a piece of fruit in exchange." He nodded toward the Model T. "Next time, pull over to the side when he comes down the street."

I knew how hard the mill employees worked and realized how important that old man and his horse were. How horrible I felt! Our family's used materials would never be thrown away again. This Rag Man was keeping the workers of the mill in jobs; the mill was the core of the town and the workers and owners were being hit by hard times, too.

The following week I waited by the side of the road with my own handful of used dish rags. As the Rag Man passed, he handed me a bunch of bananas, which were as good as gold to me.

In the 1930s, during the Great Depression, donations of rags helped to clothe the population of Massachusetts and keep the mill workers in jobs. It was a time when a simple man, equipped with just a horse and cart, could help a community survive a difficult time.

"You ready to go?" my husband asked, waking me from my daydream.

"Yes," I responded sadly, though I was not yet ready to let go of the past.

He started the car and I bid farewell to my old farmhouse. As we passed, I saw a sight that seemed so appropriate—dishtowels unfurling in the breeze on the new owner's clothesline—and a smile crossed my lips. Old towels and rags would always be important in my hometown and the Rag Man would forever be a true American Legend. ⤳

Down the Lane of
My Sweet Memories

by Sylvia Bright-Green | *Ashippun, Wisconsin*

AFTER THIRTY-FIVE YEARS OF MIND TRAVELING to the farm days of my youth, I finally returned to visit the old farmstead. The farmstead my family of fourteen brothers and sisters always referred to as Bright Acres was named upon our move to this Rock River farm near Ashippun, Wisconsin, when I was in my early teens some fifty-three years ago.

As I drove down the long dirt road to the farm of those poignant teen years, I noticed the house was unoccupied and in a state of decay. My heart saddened. This house was where I had shared dozens of memorable moments with my family. Most notable were the holidays when we all gathered around the ten-foot table laden with homegrown, farm-raised foods; foods my mother preserved from her garden to help get us through to the next growing season.

Thinking of her garden, I exited my car to view her sanctuary of love, labor, and contemplation, and couldn't find it. The field adjacent to her garden was being used to grow corn, but the rest of the land was overgrown with weeds, which buried the Garden of Eat'en setting that she meticulously planted each spring and faithfully tended through to harvest. I can still hear her say, "If you take nutrients from the soil, you return those nutrients with a compost of the same value for your next seasonal planting, or your vegetables will not nourish or flourish."

Remembering how she so loved that garden, tears filled my eyes. In anguish, I turned away and came face-to-face with the barn. The barn, where my nine brothers and four sisters and I used to play in the hayloft, was partially collapsed. Turning from that sorrowful scene, I saw the chicken coop door unlatched and banging in the breeze. The milk house, corn crib, and the tool shed were now homes to birds and other wild creatures.

Pangs of remorse tugged at my heart, and tears spilled forth. This was not the farm of my youth, I thought, as I walked around trying to find something, just anything, from my past that wasn't lost to the grasp of neglect and decay.

Finding nothing, I sadly walked back to my car. Just as I was about to open the door, a scene flashed to mind. In my disappointment I had forgotten about the place I cherished most in the whole world! My pulse quickened and my heart skipped as I ran toward the Rock River, which meandered between two fields on the south end of the 200-acre farm. As I neared the river, I saw my sweet country lane and hastened forward. When I reached the entrance, I paused and my heart took flight. The lane appeared unchanged. It was still in its natural state, as if time had stopped to await my arrival. And its beauty was more stirring than I had remembered, with all those old, canopied trees forming a church steeple along the path. This was the home of my young heart, the link to my world of make-believe, and to my world of reality.

The dirt lane still retained its ruts from the farm wagons and the horses' hooves, just as I remembered. Even the sun accommodated me by filtering through some of the tree boughs, giving the appearance of windows opening up to daily life during those days of yesteryear.

In bygone days, this country lane was our highway. It connected us to main roads, to town, to church, to our fields, and to our neighbor. The only people familiar with the lane's existence was our family and the neighboring farm. No one else was ever told about it because we didn't want it overpopulated, and because we considered it private land where we picnicked on special occasions. It was where I rode my bicycle and Blackie, our horse. It was where I came to be alone when I was sad, happy, or needed some thinking time. This lane was where my father taught me things he felt I needed to know to survive as a girl in a boy's world. Things such as how to bait a hook, climb a tree, and drive a tractor.

"Knowing these things," Dad would say, "will also help to serve you in the adult world, as well." To give an example, he would add, "Being able to drive gives you independence, knowing how to bait a hook means you will never go hungry, being skilled at climbing a tree teaches you how to mount every challenge you're going to encounter in life. So let's say that the tree is the obstacle," Dad would elaborate. "Gather your courage and move forth doing what you think and feel is best, using what you have to work with. If you fail, keep trying. But always look for the gift in the learning while you are attempting to succeed."

At that time, I didn't understand a word he said. But what I did understand was that my father wasn't a man who minced words. His advice helped me walk through many rough times in my life, times that could have had me deeply depressed. Yet due to my parents' notable influence on my young life, I was given the courage to endure anything—including the declining condition of my old farmstead—by using courage to perceive the gift in everything. In this case it was the gift of all the sentimental memories that time cannot erase. If I had had more time, I would have liked to find out who was maintaining my memory lane.

Instead, I mentally recorded the Bright Acres of my youth deeper into my heart. Now, whenever I want to harvest the way of life that seeded the person I am today, all I have to do is think about Bright Acres and it all comes back to me in a flash. ❧

Water Witch

by Anna Abrams | *Hansel Valley, Utah*

JUST PAST SNOWVILLE, UTAH, across the foothills to the south, is Hansel Valley, our destination. We have come to visit—perhaps for the last time, since this is my ninety-second year of life. The dusty, winding road leads to the dry farm where I grew up. I thrill at being home again. It feels good. I can't recall when I was last here, it's been so long.

Life on the old homestead was both a trial and a reward. Taming the wild, unbroken sod into new production was the challenge of our lives, but seeing the results of our hard work left us with a feeling of joy at our accomplishments.

My family moved to this sage- and grass-covered homestead in 1910, one year before I was born. The homestead had been secured; the humble frame home, meager sheds, a few necessary horse-drawn implements, and three sturdy workhorses were the beginnings. Unnecessary brush and grass had been railed and piled up for burning. Slowly but steadily, the soil was being turned into productivity by man, beast, and iron plow.

I remember as a small child of five how I stood on the wooden porch shading the doorway into our modest two-room shack. On the north side of the building leaned a ladder leading to the attic. Inside, a large quilt partitioned the attic into two sleeping areas— one for my brother Rudy's bed, the other side for my sister, Ella, and me.

Since we had not yet drilled for water, that precious commodity had to be hauled in each week from a well located four miles from the homestead. The well was owned and controlled by the state of Utah, drilled to accommodate a handful of sheep ranchers and cattlemen who used the area as summer pasture. The well was located on an already-cleared plot of ground where a caretaker and his wife lived. They were a kind, sociable couple named Bill and Annie Greaves. I always enjoyed seeing them since it was on those water-hauling trips that we were able to socialize and get bits of news and gossip.

Each week we drove to the well with eight wooden barrels stacked on a wagon drawn by a team of horses. The water was free and the well was deep, with a huge water tank rising high above it. We pulled the load of empty barrels alongside the tank, then waited while a spout was lowered into the barrels. The caretaker then turned a huge wheel that let the precious water flow. Afterward, we made the long journey back to the homestead over rut-filled roads as the precious water sloshed around in the barrels.

That water, more precious than gold, would serve our household, a flock of chickens, and the workhorses. Mother saved the dirty dishwater for the few sprigs of Virginia creeper vine she tried to get started to shade the bare walls of our home from the intense summer sun. The vines never did survive.

Our homestead was a half section of land located in the center of the valley. After the first strip of land was cleared and our modest home built, it was discovered that spring snow melt-offs from the surrounding hills would send torrents of water roaring into the valley, flash flooding the land where our little home stood. A well driller had tried to put down a well there but, after a few days of drilling, part of the drill bit broke off and lodged at the bottom of the hole. It could not be retrieved. No choice left except to abandon the well. And, with the flooding situation as it was, it was decided to move the house to higher ground.

We needed water badly, so another well drilling was scheduled. Before that could happen—whether by accident or by appointment, I don't know which—a man showed up at the ranch. He said he was a water witch. In his hands he held a green peach twig. As he strode over certain parts of the land, the twig would twitch when it detected water down below. He walked all around in various locations until the branch began twitching vigorously. That marked the spot to drill. My dad had faith in the man because he said he had had lots of success. A well was drilled on the very spot designated by the water witch and, at 305 feet, precious water came bubbling forth.

Now that I am older, I have my faith and I have my doubts. I wonder . . . did the peach branch contain some magical power? Was the water witch for real? Did the man possess some mental or physical properties that made the twig work, or was it only an old-fashioned fantasy to entice eager water-seeking farmers? I think back. Yes, it was for real, and I was a witness. My mind's eye still sees that ordinary man passing the peach branch back and forth over the ground as my parents anxiously watched. The sudden twitching of the branch made for a very jubilant family. We later witnessed the drill bit bringing up the stream of cold, pure water from deep within the earth at the very spot where the water witch said the water would be.

Over eighty years later, we stand at that same well, a short distance from the old farmhouse. I truly marvel that the tall steel towers still stand over the well and gentle breezes still move the windmill blades around and around, turning the huge wheels that pump the water from deep within the earth. I move closer and reach for the tin dipper hanging on a hook. My fingers tremble as I turn the faucet handle. Cold, sweet water fills the emptiness of the dipper. I smile up at my son, raise the cup in salute, then drink to my heart's content. ⤳

Another Way Home

by Christy Lanier Attwood | *Austin, Texas*

FIGHTING FOR AIR, I SHOT UP IN BED. After my last alarming episode with asthma, I promised to tell Mom the minute my symptoms began. Our recent move to the lake in Spicewood put us forty miles from the Austin hospital, and Mom wanted to make sure we had enough time to get there in case one of my frequent attacks became severe.

I found her in the bathroom, removing the bobby pins she wore at night to make her hair curly. "I'm sick, Mom." The raspy words scraped my throat.

Mom dropped the hairpins and spun around. When she squatted and pulled me close, her brown springy curls tickled my nose. I loved Mom more than anyone, but the embrace smothered me. I pushed away with a wheeze.

"Oh, sweetie, you sound horrible. Did you use your puffer?"

"No, ma'am." A rattle deep in my lungs punctuated my shallow breathing.

Mom reached into the medicine cabinet and handed me the spare inhaler. I took two puffs. "No school for you today, young lady." She guided me to the couch and propped two throw pillows behind my head. "Goodness, I don't know what to do. There's no way I can take off work again. I think I better give Nanny a call and see if you can stay with her. I have to drive into town anyway."

Sick or not, I was happy. Visiting Nanny was always a treat, and since we'd moved away from Austin, I rarely got the chance to see her.

I changed from my pajamas into a white blouse, dungarees, bobby sox, and loafers. I gathered my long hair into a ponytail and returned to the living room where Mom hollered at my brother and sisters, who were experts at dawdling.

"There'll be no Mouseketeers on TV this afternoon if you don't get moving." Her threat worked. In no time, my siblings had eaten, dressed, and were out the door with Dad. Mom and I left shortly thereafter. On the way, she reached over to squeeze my hand. "When I'm sick, all I want to do is stay home."

"It's okay, Mom." She didn't need to be sad. Nanny's house was like my second home.

Once we arrived, Mom parked on the street and we walked down the sidewalk to the screen door. Nanny's voice, sweet as sugar cookies, greeted us. "Oh, my land, look who's come to visit." Mom yanked on the flimsy door, which flew open at the top and stuck at the bottom. Out rolled Nanny's laughter, and for the millionth time she said, "That ornery thing. I've got to replace it." She gently pushed the door open and I stepped inside.

Mom joined in the laughter as she eased the door in place. She chatted with Nanny for a while, then blew me a kiss and turned to go.

"Feeling under the weather today, dear?" Nanny asked.

"Yes, ma'am." I gave a demo, complete with a wheeze and cough.

"Well, I'm sorry being sick got you here, but it's sure nice to see you." As Nanny cupped my face in her hands, the smell of gardenias wafted from her wrists. "Think iced tea might help?"

I nodded, pleased. No one could make tea like Nanny.

From the kitchen table, I watched her fill two Mason jars with fresh-brewed tea, sugar, and ice. Weeks before, I'd heard Mom say Nanny was seventy-five, which I thought sounded really old. To my eyes though, she looked as pretty in her pink-flowered dress as she ever had. Her silvery light-brown hair, which fell to her waist when she let it down, was plaited and pinned into a neat coil at the back of her head.

"I'll be right back," she said. In a flurry, Nanny headed out the side door and returned with a handful of fresh mint, which she ran under the cold-water faucet. She nudged a few green leaves into each jar and bruised them with a silver teaspoon to release the flavor. Giving the drinks a stir, she offered me one. With the first fragrant sip, I instantly began to feel better.

Nanny suggested we take our tea to the outside porch, where we sat in weathered-wood chairs, facing the huge oak tree. She claimed the "gnarly old man" had been around longer than Methuselah, which was her way of saying the tree was ancient.

When I was three, I used to recline on the lowest branch, which swept the ground. From there, I'd study the older kids as they scrambled up the tree like squirrels. In no time, I was right behind them. After six years of practice, I knew the graceful giant's every limb.

Idly, I draped one arm over Nanny's lap. Without a word, she ran her long fingernails back and forth from my hand to my shoulder. I loved being scratched; my sisters had the bug, too. Oftentimes, at night, while Doris Day or Patty Page sang on our record player, we'd take turns back-scratching.

"Feeling any better?" Nanny asked.

"Yes, ma'am." I took a breath without a single wheeze.

"Good." She patted my arm. "Would you like chicken and dumplings for lunch?" I nodded, thinking about the tender, flat dumplings swimming in a rich broth. "Then maybe we'll take a stroll to the A&W stand. If you're feeling okay."

"Oh, boy!" I imagined the heavy frosted mug, ice dripping down its sides. The frothy root beer would burn good all the way down my throat.

Nanny always said a person just never knew when they woke up where the day would lead. She was sure right. That morning, I was almost too weak to move. Two hours later, I felt much better. I took a deep helping of oxygen, the world at my feet. Smiling up at Nanny, I leaned my head against her arm. She smiled back and continued to scratch. ᕙ

The Town Dump

by Stephen D. Rogers | *Holliston, Massachusetts*

IF THERE'S ONE EXPERIENCE that can teach you more than going away to college, it's coming home again.

In 1981, I returned home to Holliston, Massachusetts, on break from a highly competitive engineering school, to learn that the town dump was closing. Closing? How could it be closing? Every Saturday for as long as I could remember, the family had piled into the station wagon to take our trash to the dump. It was a tradition.

I soon learned that our family was not the only one to feel so strongly about this weekly custom. Someone actually organized a farewell party.

Tickets were sold at the general store to pay for paper products, decorations, and soda. The food was to be potluck and everyone was encouraged to bring enough to share. A clipboard hung on the wall next to the register so that people could sign up for specific items such as chips, cookies, and ice cream. Local companies made donations to the cause. People volunteered to direct traffic.

While I don't remember there being an essay contest, I soon found myself thinking of what I would write if there was.

Part of growing up had involved being allowed to ride our bikes farther and farther from home. First, we couldn't lose sight of the house. Then we had to stay on our street. Then we could go to the far edge of Patt's farm. Then we could go all the way to the fork. Finally, we could take a right at that fork and pedal like crazy to the dump.

On Thursdays, a label manufacturer dumped its rejects. Over the years, I'd filled bags with sheets and rolls of colored dots, holiday stickers, and name tags. I wasn't a trash picker. I was a New England Yankee.

We all were. Waste not, want not. People went to the dump with trash and returned with a rocking chair or a serviceable ironing board or an I-don't-know-what-it-is-but-I'm-sure-it-will-come-in-handy-someday type of item.

Before you ever bought anything new, or even checked the secondhand store, you visited the dump to see if someone else had discarded the specific item you needed. Trash that might prove possible treasure to someone else was always left in a clearing to the right of where we parked. That pile was for the adults. We kids were more interested in the thrill of the hunt. I uncovered many a wonderful thing during my trips to the dump.

There was always a bulldozer chugging away in the background, the grit of fine sand on your lips, and gulls screeching overhead. The place had atmosphere. Oftentimes, somewhere in the distance you'd hear somebody whoop, wonder what they found, and then search all the harder.

The farewell party was a rousing success.

Burgers and chicken were barbecued and a variety of salads were set out on tables that someone had probably liberated from this very place. There was music and dancing and the exchanging of tales. When the shadows grew long and the time finally came to leave, there wasn't a dry eye in sight, and it wasn't because of the dust. ∾

The Town of Holliston, Massachusetts

Population: 14,000

Joy in Mudville

Mudville, a small neighborhood off of the downtown district, is said by some to be quite significant to the lives of baseball lovers worldwide. For it is here, according to local legend, that Ernest Thayer's poem "Casey at the Bat" was inspired. The poem, published in the *San Francisco Examiner* in 1888, vividly describes a slugger named Casey—a ballplayer Holliston residents wholeheartedly embrace as one of their own.

According to local Holliston historians, Mudville has been a neighborhood in Holliston since 1856, long before the poem was written. And since it is a known fact that baseball is, was, and always will be played in Mudville . . . well, it's just too coincidental for Holliston residents to ignore.

Town Facts

First incorporated: Holliston, established in 1724, was named in honor of Thomas Hollis, of London, England, who was a benefactor of Harvard College.

Transportation: The first train to reach the town of Holliston arrived to great fanfare on July 4, 1847. It sparked a new era in Holliston history. Alas, as automobiles became ubiquitous, the train, as well as the short-lived trolley line of 1895 to 1920, all ended up on the scrap heap. The last passenger train passed through Holliston on a quiet Sunday afternoon in 1959. Today, Holliston is one of those towns off the beaten track and out of reach of public transportation.

Location: Twenty-six miles from Boston, thirty miles north of Providence, Rhode Island, and twenty-two miles southeast of Worcester, Massachusetts.

Places of Note

The Highland Street Forest and the Adams Street Forest, maintained by the Holliston Town Forest Committee. One forest comprises 24 acres of wooded land located on the northern end of Highland Street, in a rural area of Holliston. The second is more than 200 acres on the town's western edge, off of Adams Street. The properties have been allowed to return to their natural state and are now perfect for walking, hiking, mountain biking, horseback riding, and bird watching. Local Boy Scouts have tackled the job of marking the trails for easy access. ❧

⁂

Folks of Note

In 1940, Holliston resident Arthur Moore invented a wonderful little item called the wax paper cutter box.

Country singer Jo Dee Messina, born and raised in Holliston, appeared on the music scene in the 1990s with hit songs *Heads Carolina, Tails California; I'm Alright;* and *That's the Way.* Among other honors, Jo Dee was named the Academy of Country Music's Top New Female Vocalist of 1998.

⁂

Industry: From Shoes to Straw Hats

In the nineteenth century, Holliston was known for its many shoe and boot factories. Today, a bronze plaque, affixed to a slab of granite, rests under a pine tree on the site that once housed the John Clancy Shoe Factory. The plaque notes that in the early 1800s, there were more shoes and boots made in Holliston than anywhere else in the United States. Holliston also enjoyed a booming straw hat industry from 1830 until the 1900s. ❧

Town Legend: The Balancing Rock

The Balancing Rock, a huge boulder that overhangs a precipice, is located on Washington Street. Legend has it that President George Washington stopped by in 1789 and tried to push the large boulder over only to discover what everyone before him had already figured out: the rock wasn't moving anytime soon. ❧

I Came Home to Say Goodbye

by Mary (Szymanski) Koss | *Metz, Michigan*

MY BODY TREMBLES AS I STAND and contemplate moving to the front of the room. I know what I must do, but where has my courage gone? With the medal my mother gave me shortly before her death clutched in my hand, I ask her to help me do the right thing. As I take my first steps, I feel my knees go weak. *How can I do this?* What will I say when I get to the front of this room . . . this dreadful room? But I know what Mom would say and do, and she is with me tonight in spirit, and neither of us will forgive me if I don't say something.

Dorie Centala and I were part of the 100 residents who lived in Metz, Michigan. Nestled in a wooded area, in the northern portion of the Lower Peninsula, Metz was the perfect place to grow up in. Dorie was a New Year's baby and we were sure that made her special. I, on the other hand, was only a Scorpio and the youngest kid in our class, which, of course, gave me some notoriety, but nothing in comparison.

It quickly became apparent that Dorie—being a New Year's baby and all—was our natural born leader. And lead us she did. The

►◄o►◄

president of the United States who said he'd smoked but never inhaled had nothing on us. We smoked for years before we ever inhaled. Dorie helped us find the best butts in her mother's ashtray. Gross, perhaps, but back in the '60s, to a couple of ten- and eleven-year-old kids, it meant we were cool. My sister, Karen, and I would show up on Saturday mornings to help Dorie with her chores, then we'd pack into her itsy-bitsy bathroom with the fan on full throttle—one of us standing on the toilet seat for lack of room—puffing, never inhaling, just foolishly puffing stinky, nasty butts and blowing the smoke into the exhaust fan to destroy the evidence. Sufficiently light-headed we'd file out of the bathroom with what must have been the guiltiest looks on our faces. Then we nonchalantly moved on to our next conquest. We were cool and we knew it.

Games were seldom store-bought in those days and we relied heavily on our self-appointed leader for guidance. She was truly gifted in this department. Statue was her idea. She'd physically spin you around and around and then let go. Your role was to instantaneously turn into a statue in whatever position you landed, wherever you landed, and if that was the spruce tree, you didn't dare move. If the mood struck her, she'd wind you up with her imaginary key and you were to act out your statue character. Did I love this game? Absolutely not, but I wasn't going to be the one to say so.

We whiled away hundreds of hours—playing cards, playing Monopoly, putting together puzzles, and reading *True Story* magazines. Dorie was the card dealer and the banker. She even read the *True Story* articles to us. And why not? All the toys and magazines were hers, and it was always her house. It had to be her house. She was the youngest in a family of three girls, and Karen and I were ninth and tenth in a family of sixteen children. It made perfect sense that we went to Dorie's house to do everything.

I always wondered if she read those *True Story* magazines verbatim, or included a little bit of ad-libbing. Like I said, she turned everything we did into an adventure . . . she must have had the juiciest, most interesting versions of *True Story* in her possession, because I have never found a copy as interesting as the ones she held.

She was the leader. If you didn't accept—and believe—you could quite easily find yourself living out my Bazooka bubble gum horoscope: *While everyone is in sitting, you will be outstanding.* Peer pressure is a painful thing. Dorie was fun and I wanted to be part of that fun.

We shared kindergarten through graduation and everything in between. We were the only girls in our First Holy Communion class, and everything from trick-or-treating, Christmas shopping, learning to sew, dribbling a basketball, driving a car, and learning the facts of life was done together. We did homework together—copying off each other's papers whenever we could. We grew together, apart, and back together again. I both loved and hated her. She was my best friend and my worse foe. I aspired to be as much like her as I desired to be her exact opposite. My firsts were her firsts.

You could place fifty feet side by side and I could identify her feet. How many people do you know that well? And what about those hands with the nails bitten back into the nail beds? How many times we tried to find a cure for nail-biting, to no avail—apparently, once a nail-biter, always a nail-biter.

There were very few days that I didn't spend a portion of time with my friend.

This truly must be what a heart attack feels like, I think as I make my way forward. My chest aches. My blood is exploding through my veins, and I feel my heart beating in my throat. But I know I can do this for her.

I turn to face the gathering. They're looking, waiting. Clearing my throat several times, I begin to speak. "What can you say about someone you have slept with more times than your own husband? The adventures we had . . ."

As I share our antics with the group, I see the smiles, hear the laughter, and I know Dorie is smiling, too. ❧

Bed Check Charlie

by Kermit Bentley as told to Sue A. Bentley
Robinson Creek, Kentucky

BED CHECK CHARLIE WAS AT IT AGAIN.

When he flew over our unit on the front lines in Korea—we held our breath—no one dared to even light a match. During times like this my mind drifted back to peaceful moments spent in my old Kentucky home . . .

I was born in 1927, in Robinson Creek, Kentucky. That's not a city or a town. That's just what they called our postal route, a couple of houses on one side of the road, built on the hill behind the railroad tracks. On the other side of the road was what we called bottomland or flat land, and those houses were built on level ground. Our house was one of those perched on the side of a hill held up by posts. The way our two-room house was built, the front overlooked the road and you were looking down at everything. But if you went to the back of the house and looked out the window, the mountain stared down at you. I can still hear Daddy telling stories about lying in bed and having to get up because the house had fallen over and had to be put back up on her stilts again.

There were cracks in the ceiling big enough to see the stars at night and cracks in the floor where we swept the dirt. Our only source of heat was a coal stove in the corner of the living room, so on cold nights we pasted pages from Montgomery Wards and Sears catalogs on the walls to keep the wind from blowing through.

Money was tight and shoes were a once-a-year luxury. Many a time, we walked to our one-room schoolhouse leaving bare footprints in the snow. I carried my lunch of cornbread and milk to school in a four-pound lard bucket. I would set my pail in a cold creek that ran by the school, and by lunchtime, that milk was nice and cold. Once in a great while, I'd bring a nickel and buy my lunch, a box of ginger snaps. What a treat that was!

When I was old enough, I decided to go where the money was: Detroit. My stay was short. After only eight months, I received greetings from the president of the United States. I had been officially drafted into the Korean War.

I went to boot camp for basic training in Fort Knox, Kentucky, and took the long route to Seoul, South Korea. When I arrived, the headquarters captain interviewed me. He asked if I had done any KP duty. I said very little, so he said, "We're gonna make a gunner out of you."

I replied, "Sir, I have never even seen one of those guns, much less shoot one."

He said, "Good! We're gonna train you the way we want to."

So a truck dropped me off at the front line and I had no sooner arrived than we had a "Flash Red"—enemy aircraft was in the vicinity. Everyone jumped in a foxhole, but being that I had just got off the truck, I didn't have one dug yet, so I jumped in the hole where they burned garbage. Finally the "Flash Blue" gave the all clear and I joined my roommate in the assigned pup tent. As it turned out, he was Puerto Rican and spoke no English, and I sure couldn't speak Spanish, so there we were. I did learn how to shoot one of those 155 mm Howitzers, though. I got good at it, lining it up by eye, and wound up being a gunner sergeant.

I never did think I wasn't coming home. But I remember some close calls, like when a shell whizzed by us so fast I blinked and it was gone. They later told us that the unit below us had been completely wiped out. When I was discharged from the front line, I was sent to Colorado. And of all things, they made me platoon sergeant in charge of forty-six men. I guess they figured if I came from a mountainous state, I knew how to train other guys on those mountains. It wasn't a bad job, it wasn't bad at all.

When I was finally able to take a furlough and head back home, I met up with a buddy of mine and we decided to go uptown on Saturday. Back then, that's what everyone did. They'd get dressed up and walk around Pikeville, our county seat, all day. Everyone knew each other and it didn't matter if you were a doctor, a lawyer, or a drunk, we all spoke and exchanged conversation with each other. That's just the way it was.

On this particular Saturday, my buddy and I got all dressed up in our uniforms and were walking around town, when another soldier stopped and chatted with us. He said, "I'm gettin' married at 6 P.M. tonight. How about standin' up for me?" I hesitated and told him I didn't know anything about standin' up for anyone. He said, "That's okay. Will ya do it anyway?" There wasn't anything else to do, so I said I would.

The first thing I noticed was the photographer: a big, beautiful redhead, full of curves. After the wedding, everyone went to the best restaurant in town for a chicken dinner. When I saw that redhead wrapping up chicken to take home, I fell head over heels.

We got married in the very church where we first met, and though we now live in a small town in Michigan, we go back to the green mountains of Robinson Creek every chance we get. ༄

Across the Bay

Heather Froeschl | *Eastport (Long Island), New York*

EASTPORT, LONG ISLAND, NEW YORK, was never on the A-list of the elite. It was simply a small town where real people lived, all duck farms and watermen trying to eke out an existence. Now it is a stretch of antique stores and gift shops and watermen are few and far between.

But today our family homestead *is* a restaurant on the A-list where the wealthy sup on their way from Manhattan to the beaches of West Hampton. I can still see the shape of the old house, now converted into a dining mecca. Being on the edge of the Great South Bay, just 100 feet from the lapping waves and swishing rushes, the new owners chose to maintain the sea-captain quaintness of the place. I'm sure the spirit of Grandpa is thrilled to have the barroom where his recliner used to be, and that Grandma's spirit is happy to see clean plates when the patrons are through. She always insisted that we clean our plates.

Standing at the dock, I close my eyes and breathe in the sea. I sense the past, even with the presence of Mercedes on the clamshell driveway behind me. This small town holds on to its waterman history as I hold on to my memories. . . .

The heavy air blows my hair into a sticky, curly mess of humidity and wild sea. I don't care. I lean into the bow, feeling the spray of mist after every thump of a wave. The small workboat accepts the slap of water and sends the shock through its wooden frame and into me, a steady bumping that rocks me to a sleepy state of mind. The horizon is blurry, my eyes slit against the wetness hitting my face. Though I learned long ago to keep my mouth closed and not drink the sea, my lips are salty and I can't resist the taste.

The droning is too loud to talk, but Dad stands behind me, eyes ahead, hand on the motor. I wonder how he can stand the rumble it sends up his arm, but there is no need to worry, for the captain is in control. There is a shared exhilaration between us, a love for this feeling of gliding on the water.

All too soon the engine is dropped down a notch. The roar is still there, but not so intense. I feel the swells now as we slowly float over them and approach the barrier island, which seems to rise out of the waves in an instant.

Dad cuts the engine and we drift onto the shore. With a bump, I feel the sand beneath the boat. The sliding swish announces our arrival; it's such a quiet sound. My face feels hot. Already I miss the coolness of the spray. Adjusting to the lack of noise, I enter a peaceful haven where the gentle break of the surf is soothing, and the cry of gulls overhead is a reminder of life around me.

Hopping out into the shallows, my feet sink into the cool sand that squishes between my toes. My body feels the lack of movement and a need to run. I am tempted by the stretch of sand and with a whoop of delight take off, feet pounding depressions into the clean slate of surf-swept beach. Jumping over driftwood and a horseshoe crab, I am happy and content. The wind makes music in the grass-covered dunes that separate the bay and ocean. It is a lonely sound, making me feel one with nature.

I slowly walk back, head bent to scan my path for treasures. Beach glass is much coveted by my father and me, and jingle shells soon fill my pockets. In no time I am back at the boat. The captain and I smile at each other and make ready to dig clams in the shallow cove. We speak of all things, from wishes for pet dogs to the value of being a friend. It is an easy time, with no pressure to impress or need to cover certain topics. The conversation flows and ebbs like the tide we stand in, and then we are content to work silently side by side, digging up a cache of sea life.

With bare feet, I nudge one, toe it up a bit, then reach down to grab it. For fear of finding a crab instead of a clam, I wish I could wear sneakers in the water. On those instances, I run screaming to the shore. It takes a while to get my nerve back, and I am jealous that Dad gets to use the rake. I watch him throw it out then pull it back through the sandy bottom. He flips his catch into a bushel basket floating in a tire tube nearby. No chance of crab nips on his toes.

My exploration of the shore reaps handfuls of shells and bits of intricate driftwood. I want to take the day home with me to keep, to share with my mother and sisters. I feel heaviness in my lungs when I breathe deeply and I know I will sleep well. The sun is setting and it is time to go home. I am sad to leave my paradise, but it is not yet over. I look forward to the ride back across the bay.

On this side of the past, I open my eyes to the sunset. *Red at night, sailors delight.* Legend suggests that tomorrow will be a good day to set sail; it is a good sign. I trust that this small town, where I grew up, will survive, even if it isn't just the simple homeport of the people who live off the sea anymore. Ꮼ

This Town, My Home

by Kelley Kay Bowles | *Grand Junction, Colorado*

I HAVE ONE, MOST POWERFUL, MEMORY from my high school years in Grand Junction, Colorado. It is not a memory of hot chocolate singeing my taste buds at a football game, nor one of nervously adjusting the hoop skirts of my prom dress as I wait for the limo to arrive. What I remember is a burning desire to get the heck out of my small town. This desire spanned the majority of my high school years.

The thought that there had to be something more than this was almost overwhelming. During my senior year, I pored over college catalogs from towns that seemed to offer so much more in the way of culture and entertainment; towns that didn't have any of the same old faces I'd been seeing since second grade.

I ended up making my escape. Not across the country, but a thousand miles away, at least, to the land of fun and sun— California. I had dreams of sandy beaches and palm trees, but my small college in central California was at least 100 miles from any ocean. I had fun anyway. It was like starting over. Nobody there knew what a nerd I'd been in elementary school, reading books on the playground instead of playing foursquare or tetherball, nor did they associate me with the pom-poms I'd waved and flaunted at sports events in high school. (I'd decided by then that being known as an airhead cheerleader was an improvement over nerd status.)

By the time I left my hometown, I was ready to create a new identity. California offered that chance. I combined my social and studious natures, and by the time I graduated as a teacher I felt well on my way to becoming "the me" I wanted to be. It was interesting, though. Every time I came home from college, for Christmas or to work during the summer, driving home to Grand Junction felt like a bit of peace had descended upon me. Driving through the town of Fruita where my old high school was, brought back memories of how nice it had been to know and be known by everyone. Pulling up to my mom and dad's house always filled me with a sense of tranquility, and knowing where to turn to get to the mall, or to a favorite restaurant, was strangely comforting. I'd forgotten how, when you walked down Main Street, people smiled and nodded and said hello even when you were a stranger.

I'd forgotten how nice everyone was. And a teaching position—written just for me—at my old high school, was only one of many nice things done on my behalf when I moved back home. Another nice thing that happened to me was having my former algebra teacher, whom I remember as the scariest man alive, give me a hug and a "we're glad you're here" on my first day.

But I didn't see the heart of this town in all its glory until I was diagnosed with multiple sclerosis in 1994. The shock and heartache of that diagnosis were allayed somewhat by the fact that I was here with family and friends. Their love, guidance, and just being there when I felt icky have helped me survive the past ten years.

The support of my family and friends notwithstanding, a January 1998 event sold me on Grand Junction. My new job had the added joy and responsibility of being drama director. I was in the auditorium doing a warm-up, which was a backrub circle, with the cast when my friend Lisa came to ask me a question about the set. She saw me break away from the circle and walk toward the stage in a jerky pattern, staring up at the ceiling. When she realized I wasn't doing an acting exercise, she vaulted the stairs and caught me as I collapsed in a grand mal seizure.

I awoke stretched out in the side hallway, my head on Lisa's lap as I stared into the kind eyes of my principal. He and another administrator smiled and talked soothingly as I was loaded onto the gurney, and Lisa rode with me to the hospital. The paramedic smiled and talked soothingly when I batted away the oxygen mask, my brain still residing on an electrically shorted-out planet. My neurologist smiled and talked soothingly when I awoke in the hospital room from another seizure and cried with the fear of someone who didn't know where she'd been.

My parents, of course, sat in chairs at the foot of my bed the whole time I was there. Other people—some I knew well, some I hardly knew at all—filed through my room to express their concern. The pastor of my church, in the ultimate act of forgiveness for my Christmas and Easter *only* attendance, came and held my hand, kissed my cheek, offered his time and help.

Everyone offered their time and help. This offering has been extended my way every moment of every day since then. It's helped me get through long workdays and stressful situations. And now that I've grown into a successful teacher and spokesperson for the National MS Society, I see this caring and concern exemplified by people all over this town. This town, the one I thought had nothing to offer—the town I couldn't wait to escape from—is the very town I'm so glad I came home to. ∽

Return to the Lamb

by Cindy Emmet Smith | *Wilton, New Hampshire*

IT HAD BEEN QUITE A FEW YEARS since I had been back to New Hampshire, but the road was familiar, and when the old wool mill loomed on the horizon, I knew I was near the town of Wilton. As I crossed the bridge over the Monadnock River and made the turn onto Abbot Hill Road, I was almost home.

Turning at the sign that read High Mowing, and guiding the car around the curving gravel driveway, I came to rest in front of my grandmother's home, a crucible of memories for my cousins and me.

Bought as a summer residence in the '30s, Grandma had transformed High Mowing into a school during World War II, managing to circumvent the building's moratorium and any difficulties in obtaining supplies or workmen. In the '50s and '60s, it was a gathering place for family reunions, the dormitories flinging wide their doors to accommodate any number.

It no longer looked the way I remembered from childhood summers when I ran barefoot in the coarse grass with my cousins, spun on the merry-go-round, and clambered up the smooth metal ladder into the oak tree. Part of that venerable tree had been scorched by the fire that devoured the buildings in 1970, but I could still taste the watermelon we ate and feel the slick seeds I held in my mouth, poised to shoot at the nearest laughing face.

I smiled at the big, flat, granite rock that still reserved its place of honor as the doorstep. Inside, the stairs did not lead up mural-painted walls to hidden bedrooms tucked beneath the plastered eaves, furnished with plump feather comforters, but only to three tidy guestrooms and a modern bath.

I tossed my bag onto the nearest bed and opened the window, letting the smell of newly cut hay drift in from the neighboring farm. As I made my way downstairs to have dinner with my grandmother, I watched fireflies prick light into the darkening yard.

"So, you plan on getting married here?" Grandma asked, her smile reaching across the table.

"As long as it's okay with you."

"And this is the right fellow."

Now it was my turn to smile. "Yes, he is."

"You know, there have been many weddings here on the hill, but you're the first of my grandchildren to get married here."

"Actually, I've always wanted to. I used to imagine pictures of the wedding party reflected in the pool."

Grandma shook her head. "I don't think that will be possible in December."

"My next idea is to have the wedding in the chapel and the reception in the Big Room. You did rebuild the chapel, didn't you?"

"Yes, it was one of the first things we did."

I closed my eyes and remembered. "The old one was so pretty . . . dim and solemn with that dark paneling and those beautiful stained-glass windows."

"The windows will look familiar. A former student made reproductions from old photos." She sighed, her eyes taking on a faraway look. "So many people did things like that after the fire."

Glad that people had rallied around her, I exclaimed, "How wonderful! That's why the place feels the same, even if the buildings look different."

"I'm glad you think so. It's been only five years, but the school has risen from the ashes like the Phoenix," she said proudly.

I smiled back at her. "Mom wanted me to make sure everything looked nice enough for a wedding."

"Look around all you want. But keep in mind, there's more to a wedding than the place."

I nodded, then shot her a pensive look. "Do you think they'll come? The cousins and uncles and aunts?"

She smiled encouragingly. "I think I can even persuade Beulah."

Beulah, my Aunt Boo, lived in Switzerland and hadn't seen all her brothers in over twenty years. I knew it would take a lot to persuade her to make the long trip.

"If anyone can do it, you can, Grandma."

The next day, in the late-summer heat, I wandered across the slumbering grounds. With no one to fill and maintain the pool, it stood empty. I admired its natural bedrock floor as I passed. A few faculty members made the hill their year-round residence and I greeted the ones I remembered.

I saved the chapel for last. It was lovely—a small room with pine benches, whitewashed walls, and bright new woodwork. A wrought-iron chandelier hung from the ceiling, and matching candle stands stood on the mantel flanking a small stone lamb. The lamb had traveled from ancient China years ago. It had withstood the devastating fire that had all but destroyed High Mowing. It had always graced the chapel, its fleece polished by the loving touch of many fingers. Many of those fingers belonged to my family.

I had a catch in my throat as I thought about my family. The family ties had grown thin of late, stretching around the globe, but they were still strong enough to bind us together forever. I stroked the smooth stone and wondered if those ties were strong enough to gather everyone for my wedding.

As I walked down the aisle of that small chapel, some months later in my wedding gown, my eyes grew misty. They had all come. My wedding, our grandmother, this chapel, the lamb that graced its altar, and these sacred grounds had sent out a call none could resist. We had asked them to come home and they did. ∽

The Pilot and the Paperboy

by David Crane Swarts | *Rushville, Indiana*

EVERY SMALL TOWN HAS ITS HEROES, and Rushville, Indiana, is no exception. One of our heroes is Joe Cotton—we've even named a street after him.

I remember the first time I heard his name. It was a hot, sunny, summer afternoon. I was ten years old and delivering *The Rushville Republican.* I heard this rumbling roar from the air, and as I looked to the sky, mouth agape, I saw a huge jet aircraft in a slow circular bank. It was a B-52 bomber, I knew, having built model airplanes, and it was so low that it seemed to just miss the treetops when it turned. I asked my mother when I returned from my paper route if she saw the airplane.

"Oh, yes," she chuckled. "That's Joe Cotton showing off again."

My mother and the then Major Cotton were contemporaries. Joe Cotton flew bombers in World War II, was shot down, avoided capture, and returned safely home without a scratch. He stayed in the Air Force and happened to be stationed at Wright Patterson AFB, in Dayton, Ohio, when I caught my first glimpse of him, or rather the behemoth of an airplane he was flying, in 1959. He took great delight in buzzing the town and everyone watched the private air show with pride, for one of our own was flying by.

Two years later, I switched from the evening paper route to a morning route delivering *The Indianapolis Star.* Two years after that I had a new customer, Ella Cotton, Joe's mother. In the meantime, Joe had been reassigned to Edwards AFB in California as a test pilot for the XB-70, the prototype for the present-day B-1 bomber, and had flown the maiden flight as aircraft commander.

Paperboys collected the money from subscribers in those days, and I collected on Saturdays. Mrs. Cotton took a shine to me and often invited me in to chat, usually about God and the importance of being born again. She was a dyed-in-the-wool Baptist. I could always count on spending at least an hour before I would be paid and on my way. One Saturday, Mrs. Cotton had a letter from Joe that she was just bursting to share with me. Now we're getting someplace, I thought. I had read in *The Star* just a week earlier how Joe had averted a catastrophe during a test flight in his plane named Cecil. There had been two airplanes, Cecil and Cecilia, so named because the planes looked like sea serpents and Cecil was the name of a cartoon sea serpent at that time.

Dear Mother,

I'm sure by now you've read about what happened on my last flight. Not to worry though, the problem has been analyzed six ways to Sunday and repairs are now being made to Cecil. As we were about to land, our instruments indicated that the landing gear would not go down. The onboard computers prevented us from lowering the gear because the gear doors were jammed. Fortunately, we had fuel for about an hour of flight left. I studied the circuits in the manual for the logic, and found that if I shorted the circuits in a certain way, the *computer would "think" that the gear doors were open and we could force the landing gear down. We had about thirty minutes of flying time left when I disassembled the circuitry and jumpered the circuits. Sure enough the landing gear forced the doors open and was now locked in place. I didn't hold the jumper on long enough, however, to unlock the brakes on the wheels. A couple of seconds more would have done it. So when we landed, we blew every tire on the airplane and skidded down the runway with every tire on fire. I ruined all four of the struts that go from the wheels to the fuselage, each of which costs $250,000. As you know, we all safely returned. We test pilots surely lead exciting lives, and I had the strange sensation that you were praying for me. Were you?*

> *Love,*
> *Joe*
> *P.S. Sorry about your tax money.*

"Exciting? That's downright dangerous, in my opinion!" Mrs. Cotton said as she shook her head.

"So . . . were you?" I asked.

"Was I what?"

"You know . . . praying for him?"

"I pray for him every day. I'll have to check the exact time when all this was happening to him," she said, pondering the thought.

"I don't think you have to check," I said with a wink as I made for the door. "And I don't think you're upset about the tax money, either!"

Mrs. Cotton just smiled.

Now whenever I return to Rushville, I have to pass the house where Mrs. Cotton lived. And when I do, I always remember when I was a paperboy sitting at her feet, listening to her read Joe's letters and of this grand old lady reminding me of the power of prayer. ᐰ

Gatherings Remembered

by Janet Shaub White | *Grayslake, Illinois*

As the women's circle meeting ended, I walked to the wastebasket and discarded my dessert plate and cup. But instead of dropping the lavender paper napkin into the trash receptacle, I ran my fingers across the stylized yellow blossoms along the borders and slowly walked back into my friend's cozy living room. The buzz of conversations faded away and I was enveloped in a cloud of tender memories.

Often, when my mother returned from her church circle meetings, women's club, or other such gatherings, she brought a delicate paper napkin home with her in her handbag. If I weren't home from school yet, she left the napkin out to show me. Afterward, she opened the heavy mahogany drawer in the dining room buffet, and patted the napkin down onto the top of a bed of others. No two alike, odd souvenirs, like some people might collect matchbooks. They would not be reused; they were there only for the handling and the remembering.

Those dainty napkins told a tale, a record really, of my mother's simple social life. They represented her circle of connectedness, mainly with women from church. We lived in Grayslake—back then a small town of 5,000—in the heart of Lake County, Illinois. I knew almost everyone in my graduating class; I knew where they lived and who their siblings were. Farm life went on around us, but it was less important with each passing year. The train station was gradually becoming more active with commuters to Chicago. Grayslake was a town in transition.

From time to time, my mother opened the drawer and fingered those pretty paper napkins as though counting, but more likely recalling, each hostess and event. I rarely witnessed those gatherings, as they were held during the daytime when school was in session, but the evidence was right there in the drawer. And when it was my mother's turn to host, she planned and prepared all week. Sometimes I helped her polish the silver-plated teaspoons and dessert forks. Sometimes I helped prepare the dessert or taste a sample of a brand-new recipe.

The night before, she covered the table and heavy brown table pad with a freshly pressed ivory or white damask cloth. Sometimes she draped a lacy tea-colored tablecloth atop the linen. Then she patterned the forks and spoons, often in a double crescent, but sometimes zigzagging them at one corner of the table. Next she placed her china cups and saucers, either those with tiny pink roses or the celadon maple leaf–patterned ones, and one of several sets of dessert plates. My favorites were hand-painted, each with a different flower, a misty pastel background, and a golden rim. She usually put out two sets of cream pitchers and sugar bowls, one by the coffeepot and the other next to the teapot.

Last, she would lay out the small paper napkins, the only disposable items on the table. No paper packets of sugar. No plastic forks or spoons. No store-bought dessert in aluminum. And those napkins were neither plain nor selected without consideration. They would represent the season or a color theme she had chosen. Like the silverware, she would lay them in a pleasing pattern. I delighted in seeing them. After all, paper products were a luxury in those times. We used cloth napkins at all our family meals, and Mother set a beautiful table, with small touches like condiments in their own little dishes, with their own tiny spoons. But when the ladies were coming over, she could be a bit extravagant; delicate paper napkins added just the right touch.

The day of the meeting, she picked a rose from her garden and dropped it into one of her rose bowls for the centerpiece. Or she placed pansies in a flower ring, or chose a porcelain figurine or a cut-glass fruit bowl for the centerpiece. Whichever, it would be just right, a still-life setting worthy of a painter's brush.

I've been gone from Grayslake for quite a few years now, but memories don't really fade away. I think they drift off to a special storage place, gently padded with time and love. There they await just the right occasion to unwrap themselves and revisit. My community now is tiny Green Lake, Wisconsin, where life centers around the state's deepest lake and the population of 1,100 doubles when the summer folks come. Church circles and other service groups are still a vital force in women's lives here, and in my own life. We usually gather in the evenings now, after getting home from work, and likely will have to drive farther than my mother did in order to get together.

Trips back to Grayslake, just three hours south, are infrequent, since family and closest friends are now gone. But when I do pass through, it's fun to recall the familiar and note the changes. The schools all have additions, the farmlands closest to town are new neighborhoods quaintly named in an effort to capture some of the charm of bygone days, and the stores no longer bear surnames of people we knew. There are more choices of churches, of garden centers, of hair salons. My mother's was in her friend's basement, where just the two of them could swap stories of family triumphs and troubles. Instead of a single street of shops, there are numerous strip malls near those farms turned into building sites. Grayslake has burst out of its small-town cocoon and transformed into a bustling suburb.

Blinking back to the present, I notice it is getting late and time to leave this comfortable gathering of friends. I bid my hostess goodbye and gently tuck the lavender souvenir into my purse. ∿

The Town of Grayslake, Illinois

Population: 18,506

Historical Timeline

1836—First settled.

1842—William Gray bought land, including part of Gray's Lake.

1886—Grayslake was platted as a subdivision.

1953—Lake County Fairgrounds moved to its current location at US 45 and 120.

1969—College of Lake County opened its doors.

1970—Grayslake celebrated its Diamond Jubilee.

1985—Grayslake celebrated its centennial with year-long activities.

First incorporated: 1895

Famous Grayslake Residents

Swee' Pea, Miss Dog USA 2003, is a resident of Grayslake, residing at TOPS in Dog Training Kennels with her owners Alex and Paula Rothacker. Alex (a.k.a. "Popeye") and his amazing dog trick act have performed throughout the United States and Canada since 1984, including recent appearances on both *The David Letterman Show* and *The Tonight Show with Jay Leno*, where the voting public voted Swee' Pea the "Smartest Dog in the World."

Location: The Village of Grayslake, located in Central Lake County between Chicago and Milwaukee, is approximately forty miles north of the Chicago business "Loop," and fourteen miles west of Lake Michigan. Nearby communities to Grayslake include: Libertyville, Mundelein, Gurnee, Lindenhurst, Round Lake, and Round Lake Beach. The distance from Grayslake to Washington, D.C., is 649 miles. The distance to the Illinois state capital is 197 miles.

Places of note: Gray's Lake, a seventy-eight-acre recreational lake, is located within the boundaries of the village. Its central location puts residents within a fifteen-minute drive to major regional shopping centers, several golf courses, the Chain of Lakes and Lake Michigan marinas, beaches, state parks, hundreds of acres of forest preserves, and winter skiing and snowmobiling, as well as the Great America amusement park and the world-famous Ravinia Outdoor Music Festival.

The heart of Grayslake is the village center, including the historic downtown with its antique lighting, historic storefronts with varying architectural styles, and small businesses that are customer-friendly.

Grayslake has many unique facilities that set it apart from other communities and enhance the reputation of the village. The College of Lake County, the Lake County High School Technology Campus, and the Center for Economic Development, with their extensive personnel training and business services, are located in Grayslake. The College of Lake County has a consistent enrollment of more than 15,000 students.

The Village of Grayslake is the proud home of the Lake County Fairgrounds, which hosts one of the most popular annual county fairs in Illinois. The Lake County Fair and various events held annually at the fairgrounds throughout the year draw more than 500,000 people to Grayslake from all over the Midwest. Some of these events include: antiques and collectibles shows, computer shows, antique car shows and swap meets, and animal shows.

The Soldier in the Gold Frame

by Peggy Vincent | *Wilmington, Delaware*

VERY EARLY THE NEXT MORNING, my daddy would leave to go to war.

It was 1944. Although I was barely two, I remember the walk we took, just my tall, lanky father and me. On that cold autumn day, we ambled down the country road to a pasture to feed carrots to an enormous, but gentle, old horse. Appearing as soon as my dad made a clicking sound with his tongue, the horse stretched his neck to sniff the carrots in my hand. My father picked me up, and I watched in fascination as huge yellow teeth appeared when the horse's fleshy lips rolled back.

I don't recall any conversation that day. I just remember putting my arm around my father's shoulder and feeling the roughness of his military jacket with my bare hand, then letting the horse take the whole carrot so it freed my other hand to touch, in wonder, the strangeness of tears on my father's cheek.

During the eighteen months he was gone from us, Mommy and I lived with my grandparents in a row house in Wilmington, Delaware. At naptime and bedtime, my mother held a photograph of my father in his army uniform for me to kiss. I stood up, stamped my feet, and played peek-a-boo with the photo, turning and twisting like a hula dancer—anything to avoid kissing him. Once I'd pressed my lips to the cool glass in the frame, I would have no excuse to avoid going to sleep.

But my mother was relentless, and every way I turned, the picture was there: a thin-faced soldier in uniform, wearing a creased cap and a shy, proud smile. During that war, men really believed they were fighting for God, country, and their families back home. My dad's faith shines from the photo, which, almost sixty years later, still rests in the same thin gold frame on my mother's dresser.

When Japan surrendered, my father, along with hundreds of thousands of other fortunate soldiers, was sent home. He spent several weeks in Hawaii and San Francisco waiting for his ticket to travel by train across the country toward home, his parents and wife, and a child who might not even remember him.

My mother, giddy with excitement, took me into New York to meet his train. Gripping her hand, I felt the energy of the crowds around me on the rain-slick streets. We surged on the crest of a wave of women, of all ages, hurrying to bring their men home from war. The women wore dresses whose shortness became a fashion statement due to the scarcity of fabric: fitted slim skirts, snug jackets that flared a bit below the waist, wide lapels, and blouses with cutwork embroidery. All of the women wore hats with a slanted brim, some with a feather sticking out at a proud angle.

Once inside the station, we met an outgoing tide of people and noise, and men in uniform. The heady smell of cigarettes, new clothes, train grease, old newspapers, damp wool, and sausages filled the air. Crackling loudspeaker announcements echoed off the impossibly high ceiling, but in the din of thousands of joyful people, no one appeared to be listening. The sea of people flowed onward.

A logjam of humanity hemmed us in, and then we popped to the front of a river of women at a wide flight of stairs. It looked dangerous, but I was thrilled with the risk as the current somehow carried me toward the bottom, wedged between hips, thighs, tweed, and damp raincoats, my feet scarcely touching the ground. Amazed that Mommy's hand still clutched mine when we hit bottom, I looked at the long, concrete platforms between the trains and wondered how we would ever find my father.

After staring at a huge chalkboard of numbers, my mother planted herself beside what she assured me was my daddy's train.

Women with young children in their arms, or pulling those big enough to walk, ran back and forth as fast as their high heels would permit, scanning the soldiers leaping off the trains with huge duffel bags slung across their backs. The bags swung dangerously close to those feathered hats as the soldiers, too, strode up and down the platforms looking for certain faces in the crowd. Great billows of steam puffed beneath the trains and sizzled as it dripped on hot tracks. The odors of oil and dusty upholstery, so many unwashed men and perfumed women, the screaming train brakes, and the crash of metal couplings slamming together were all a confusing background medley to the joyful din of yelling people, crying children, screams of joy, shouts of victory.

Then my mother and I were part of it as she saw her husband's face below a sharply creased hat, but above the crowd, a face far thinner than the one in the photo. She swung me onto her hip and waded through the chaos, one arm outstretched.

"Bill!" she shrieked. "Billy! Here!"

He spun left and right, then saw us and held aloft his beacon, a toy broom bought for me in Hawaii. We moved toward it, swimming upstream against the tide of bodies, while he surged downstream toward us. At last we were together. Squashed between them as they embraced, I looked over my mother's shoulder at his hand on her back, a hand with a loose wedding ring, a hand clutching a red-handled broom.

Eventually, they separated enough for me to wiggle around to face him. I stared for only a second, then leaned forward and kissed the smiling face behind the cool glass in the frame. Only this time it was warm, scratchy with unshaved whiskers, but once again wet with tears. ∾

The Girl in Charge

by Sharon Landeen | *Rock Springs, Wyoming*

ON A RETURN VISIT TO MY HOMETOWN of Rock Springs, Wyoming, I couldn't resist ordering a chocolate milkshake and taking a trip down Memory Lane. As the first sip caressed my taste buds, I smiled and remembered "the Girl in Charge." It felt like just yesterday when the '53 Buick pulled into the dusty parking lot of the diner where I was working.

"Hellooo, handsome," I whispered, looking at the Buick's driver. I checked my reflection from my saddle shoes to my ponytail in the chrome refrigerator, then turned to watch as he walked through the door. Every gorgeous hair of his crew cut stood at attention. His senior letterman sweater radiated.

"Where's Red?" he asked while I mixed his cherry Coke.

"He's not here," I answered, trying to sound casual. "I'm in charge tonight."

That was not a complete out-and-out lie, just a little embellishment. Red, my boss, had said he would be gone for forty-five minutes. Since I was sixteen and my coworker a mere fifteen, I was to be in charge. *In charge.* What an all-powerful phrase.

As he settled down with his Coke, the bell on the door jingled and in walked the two spinster sisters for their routine ice cream sundaes. After much discussion, they decided on one caramel sundae and one butterscotch sundae. My coworker gave me a look of panic when she realized our butterscotch syrup container was empty. Winking at her, I quickly put the same caramel syrup on both sundaes, covered them in whipped cream, and topped them with a cherry.

"Remember," I said sweetly, "the butterscotch sundae's the one on the right." As both sisters began eating, I realized that being in charge came to me naturally.

A car door slammed. I didn't even need to look at the out-of-state license plate; the loud shirt and the camera screamed "tourist."

"Hello there," announced an elderly gentleman. (He must have been at least fifty.) "The last time I was through your town, I had the best burger and chocolate shake here. Think your boss could fix me another?"

"Sure thing," I replied confidently. "But the boss is gone and I'm in charge tonight."

My coworker went to the back to catch up on the dishes as I smoothly slapped a burger on the grill. I nonchalantly picked up the milkshake container, put in two squirts of chocolate syrup, three scoops of ice cream, and added milk to the line on the container. Without missing a beat, I put the container on the milkshake maker and clicked it on. Turning around, I deftly flipped the burger and began to assemble the lettuce, onion, and tomato.

Nothing to this, I thought, congratulating myself. Perhaps I was too quick with my praise, because at that moment my thoughts were interrupted by an unsettling sound. My suaveness began to fade as I realized that in my haste, I had incorrectly hooked the container to the milkshake machine. Science has never been one of my strong points, but that evening I clearly saw the effects of centrifugal force. At that point, I understood the force that tends to impel things outward from the center of rotation.

Fortunately, most of my customers ducked as the first scoop of ice cream came flying toward them. Unfortunately, Mr. Tourist was not as quick. He took it in the head. The second ice cream scoop also hit the target—this time the man's loud shirt.

The third ice cream missile landed on the ceiling above Mr. Tourist, along with the remaining milk and chocolate syrup. Horrified, I jumped up onto the lunch counter, grabbed my cleanup rag, and began to mop anything within my reach . . . the ceiling, Mr. Tourist's head, his shirt, the counter. But all I managed to do was spread the sticky mess.

I must have sounded like a stuck phonograph record, repeating "I'm sorry" over and over again. Right about then the burning smell enveloped me. Climbing down from the counter, I saw that "the best burger in town" now resembled a smoking hockey puck.

It was then that my debonair "in charge" self was replaced by a totally frazzled teenager.

With a sinking feeling I realized it was very possible I was the inspiration for the term "soda jerk."

In the middle of all the chaos came a loud rumbling laugh from the doorway. The sound started deep in Red's belly and came roaring out. Red's face now matched his hair, and tears rolled down his cheeks. He soon was joined by the twittering laugh of the Sundae Sisters, the deep laugh of Mr. Handsome, and the giggle of my coworker. Mr. Tourist started to smile, and soon he and I joined the group in a laughing marathon.

I happily relinquished my title to Red.

While I cleaned up the mess, Mr. Tourist retired to the restroom to salvage what he could of his shirt. Red volunteered to have the shirt cleaned for him, free of charge, but Mr. Tourist said that he never liked that particular shirt anyway and donated it to the trashcan.

When it was time to go, Mr. Handsome said he'd see me at school tomorrow—and I knew in that instant he would remember me, which wasn't all bad. And though Mr. Tourist finished the night off in his undershirt, he enjoyed the burger Red made him, and the new milkshake, carefully made by me. I guess he wasn't too upset, because after he left I found a note under his plate that read, "For the girl in charge." Inside was a sticky, chocolate-stained $5 bill—the largest tip I had ever received. ✑

Roy Rogers and the Tent Show

by Barbara J. Burk | *Success, Missouri*

NASHVILLE IS SEVEN HOURS AWAY from my hometown of Success, Missouri. It's not an easy drive, but the panoramic vistas help alleviate the physical discomforts somewhat. At any rate, every Thanksgiving, Christmas, Fourth of July, and Mother's Day finds me on the road home. This year was my sprightly mother's eighty-fifth birthday, so on Mother's Day my sister and I drove home and picked her up, so we could treat her to a trip to the Roy Rogers Museum in Branson. Mom loved every minute of our little adventure, and I was flooded with memories—long forgotten—of my childhood, Roy Rogers, and my very first movie.

In 1946, movies were unknown in the isolated Ozark Mountains, along with running water, electricity, and phones. I was five years old and my favorite chore was accompanying Mom on the weekly three-mile trek to our local country store/post office in Success. I could usually wheedle her out of a five-cent Butterfinger, but I'd been extra good this week and hoped to hit her up for an Orange Nehi as well. Following Mom along the well-beaten path, I kept a sharp eye out for chiggers and ticks while imagining the chocolaty crunch and ice-cold tangy sweetness just minutes away.

But when we arrived, instead of the store rising into view, a huge tent appeared. I stopped short, completely speechless with mouth agape and my grandiose scheme for sweets temporarily forgotten. My amused mother read the colorful poster aloud. It was an announcement about a traveling movie show starring Roy Rogers and his Wonder Horse, Trigger, and was showing one night only. I had never seen a movie before and could hardly contain my excitement.

"Could I go? Please, please, please?" I begged. Mom exhibited considerably less enthusiasm, but joy of joys, did not say no and a tiny spark of hope began to glow. This was only morning. The movie was not until later that night. I had the whole day to plead my case.

My young but inventive brain began feverishly plotting, formulating outlandish promises for feats hitherto undreamed. For Roy Rogers I would milk the cow, strain the milk, and carry the crocks down to the springhouse. I would pound the gallon jar of cream against my spindly legs until it yielded fresh butter and tangy buttermilk for a cornbread supper. I would haul buckets of fresh spring water up the hill for drinking, cooking, and replenishing our woodburning cookstove's hot water reservoir. I would make the biscuits all week long!

"Hush!" Mom said before I irretrievably hung myself. "We'll see."

I am forever grateful Mom interrupted me at the beginning of my speech. After five years of experience with my mother, I knew that "We'll see" meant yes. I was almost too excited to eat supper. As soon as my chores were done, we filled the swinging kerosene lantern for our return trip later that night and set off. Once again, we covered the three miles to town, going over the rail fence, across the creek, and through the woods toward the traveling tent show.

I will never forget how extra special I felt that night. Mom let me wear my brand-new dress, just finished that morning. I was particularly proud because I had picked out the material myself. She had taken me with her to meet the delivery truck with its monthly shipment of chickenfeed, packed in colorfully printed cloth bags. Firmly braced against the less-than-discreet jostling from the other equally determined mothers, she successfully managed to find my chosen pattern and the required amount of material for one small dress.

Though we covered the distance twice as fast as normal, we still had to stand in a long line to pay the ten-cent admission fee. Many years later I was greatly amused to hear someone describe her fear of breaking down in the wild, isolated, and deserted backwoods area we called home. In reality, our rural neighborhood was fairly crowded, as was all too evident tonight. Even Slim Turner, the local moonshiner, whom I was forbidden to acknowledge in any way, lurked at the rear of the line.

Though few of our neighbors lived near the roadside, their homes were close—only a hill or two off the beaten path. Their close proximity was proven every morning and evening as their individually recognizable cries of "Sook, sook" and "Sooey, sooey" echoed across the valleys as they called their cows and pigs home for milking and feeding.

Finally, we were admitted through the tent flap into a dim interior, illuminated by hanging kerosene lanterns. Climbing over the extended feet and knees of the early birds, we quickly took our seats on a wooden plank braced on either end by large crates. Anticipation mounted as everyone impatiently swatted mosquitoes while waiting to behold the miracle of modern technology.

I was in heaven.

Finally, a stout middle-aged man walked around the interior, turning down the lantern wicks until near total darkness prevailed.

And at last, miracle of miracles, the movie began. I was utterly enthralled and sat frozen to my seat, quiet as a mouse, from the opening scene to the end.

Alas, it was over much too quickly. The lanterns were turned back up and everyone reluctantly found their way outside into the starlit night. Lighting our own lanterns, we began the long journey home under a glorious full moon, accompanied by the familiar chorus of whippoorwills, hooting owls, chirping crickets, and croaking frogs.

The wonders of nature, however, were totally wasted on me. I was in love. I was a million miles away, reliving the movie's every action-packed moment while Roy's melodious voice crooned soulful ballads in my ear. And I don't mind admitting that many a dream afterward featured my small self as a miniature Dale Evans held securely by Roy as we rode Trigger the Wonder Horse into the sunset. ⌒◡

Home Harbor

by Mary Norton Ross | *Wallingford, Connecticut*

LIKE A SHIP COMING INTO PORT, we would sail up to my grandfather's house in the old New England silver town of Wallingford, Connecticut. Although generations of my ancestors are buried there, I was a World War II Navy brat and had never anchored anywhere for more than two and a half years. But both my parents had gone to school, met, and married in this tree-canopied place with its historic roots that reached back beyond my lifetime. Grandpa Sorenson's two-story house, with its tall trees hemming it in on all sides—like ships' masts—was always a safe harbor for me and seemed large to a child used to military quarters or housing near a naval base.

To ensure his family had plenty of room, Grandpa had bought several lots adjoining his property. The back lots included a few trees and a large, carefully turned compost heap where all the table scraps and vegetable garden refuse turned into fertile soil. During harvest seasons, Dad would stop by Beaumont's Farm—not far from the house—for just-picked sweet corn. The corn husks were added to the compost after my brother and I finished stripping the cobs. And

Aunt Ingrid and Mom were sure to make apple pies from the fruit of the several old apple trees on the property.

On the side lot, to the right of his large garage, Grandpa built an elaborate stone grill with a chimney from the New England rocks he'd dug out of his garden. Both he and my dad, who had also been an engineer for the Connecticut Highway Department, made quite a study of stones and minerals of all kinds. Dad used to recite the old tale that when the Puritans chased the devils out of New England, they fled to Long Island and threw all the rocks back at the settlers, which is why New England is a rock-bound coast full of pebble beaches, while Long Island is practically rock-free.

Grandpa's house had enough rooms for all of us. When I woke in the mornings and had to be quiet so as not to wake the elders, I browsed the glass-covered antique bookcase in my bedroom and read the same books that my mother had read. The illustrated editions of *Ivanhoe, King Arthur, A Little Maid of Old Connecticut,* and *A Little Maid of Narragansett Bay* all asked the ancient question, "Where will you find your true love?" As a young girl, I sometimes fantasized about sailing off on a mighty ship into the sunset to find adventure and maybe my true love.

Later in the day, we'd go swimming with local people at the town's quarry pool, or Mom and Aunt Ingrid would prepare a picnic for a scenic trip. Growing up in a small town before the automobile's now ubiquitous presence, my dad loved to go for a drive and perhaps find an adventure. So he'd load Mom's picnic basket, an old Navy blanket, a portable charcoal grill, and the family into the car. Then we'd drive to some park or historical site within a day's reach.

Years passed, and I became a teen during the Korean War and met a handsome young sailor in Virginia. While I finished Adak High School in the Territory of Alaska, on a remote island in the Bering Sea, he finished his tour of duty with a helicopter squadron in New Jersey. When I returned home, I brought back a husky dog with curly coal black hair, which we'd named Adak.

Not liking the separation for so long, my sailor and I began to meet at Grandpa's house. He would drive all the way from New Jersey on his weekends off. One dark evening we had Grandpa's backyard to ourselves. A perfect time and place for romance. But just as we were happily getting reacquainted, Adak approached unseen. A wet doggie tongue, instead of me, kissed my intended. "My how you've changed!" my fiancé would say when telling of it later.

Even in home port we were seldom moored for long, and our all-too-brief vacations with grandparents were soon over. Finally, I cut the anchor and sailed off with my new husband. But forever after, home to me would be a two-story house with a porch, surrounded by tall trees that reminded me of the masts of old ships sailing back from adventures at sea.

The Green Stamp Heirloom

by Renie Burghardt | *Doniphan, Missouri*

IN THE LATE 1920S, my great-uncle Peter left Hungary and traveled to America. In 1931, he met and married Millie, a lovely American girl.

Uncle Peter and Aunt Millie were never blessed with children of their own, so when my grandparents and I came to America in the '50s, all their affections were lavished on me. Of course, as a teenager, I reveled in it. Besides, they spoke English to me, and I loved the town they lived in. Doniphan was a little rural town in the Missouri Ozarks, and much different from the noisy city where we lived.

Nestled in the beautiful, forested hills of the Current River valley, Doniphan was a magical place to visit. During all the wonderful vacations at their house, among other things, I enjoyed the bounty of Uncle Peter's vegetable garden and the beauty of Aunt Millie's flower garden. But, inside the house, an object on their fireplace mantel absolutely enchanted me. It was the most beautiful clock I had ever seen.

One day, I asked Aunt Millie where she got the clock and whether it was terribly expensive. I was hoping my grandparents could soon afford to buy one just like it.

Millie said she first laid eyes on the clock in June 1918, when she had just turned five. She was in the backyard jumping rope when suddenly she heard her mother's cries coming from the kitchen. Alarmed, Millie ran into the house asking if something was wrong.

"Oh, no dear," her mother exclaimed. "On the contrary, everything is perfect!" She motioned with her hands toward the table. "See all these filled books of Green Stamps? I have been saving them for two years, and now I finally have enough of them to get it."

"Get what, Mama?" Millie asked, caught up in her mother's excitement.

"The clock with the golden pendulum." She handed Millie the Green Stamp catalog. "Oh, Millie, wait until you see it. It's a beautiful clock, and the chimes make the loveliest sound you ever heard. It will be perfect up there on the mantel." Millie's hazel eyes gazed in wonder at the picture of the clock with the golden pendulum.

The following morning, Millie's mother was in such a hurry to get her new clock, she left the dirty breakfast dishes in the sink, something Millie had never seen her do before. By the time they reached the Green Stamp redemption store, Millie was as excited as her mother was.

As soon as they walked back through the door of their home, Millie's mother lifted the beautiful clock out of the box, set it in the center of the mantel over the fireplace, and hung the pendulum. She quickly wound the clock and moved the hands 'round the clock so they could listen to the chimes ring on the hour, then the half hour. Grinning, her mother called Central for the correct time.

Millie confided that hearing the sweet sound of chimes for the first time had been a thrill, and late at night the golden tone comforted her and made her feel safe and secure. Many years later, her mother wrapped the clock up as a wedding gift for her. How excited Millie had been to set it over her own mantel. When Millie's mother died, the golden tones comforted Millie in her great sorrow. Thinking back, she remembered her mother's smiling face again, as radiant as it had been the day Millie accompanied her to pick up the clock.

Millie told me the story in 1952. All the years since, I continued to admire the clock, so you can imagine my surprise when, in 1962, when Aunt Millie passed away, the clock with the golden pendulum was willed to me, becoming a part of my own children's lives. The only difference was that we lived in the city. It just made sense that after my children grew up and moved on to lives of their own, that the longing I had all those years to go back to beautiful Doniphan should became a reality.

Twenty years ago, I came back to these forested Ozark hills to live, and I brought the clock with me. It still keeps perfect time, and the sound is as enchanting as ever, bringing with it memories of a little girl named Millie, and sweet dreams to three visiting granddaughters. ᎒

A Chronicle of Unexpected Blessings

by Denise Nash | *Leaburg, Oregon*

I NEVER DREAMED the little country church of my childhood would weave itself into my life so fully. But as I look back now, I realize the church has always been a part of me.

The building was erected on property my grandmother had deeded to the church, and the narrow strip of land below the church that adjoined ours added to the acreage we children thought of as our playground. The church was so much a part of our family traditions that on every New Year's Eve my family, and a few friends, slipped through the darkness as midnight approached to ring in the New Year by taking turns pulling the old rope attached to the heavy bell. I loved the lazy mellow clang that followed each pull. And on Sunday mornings, Mom and I walked down the lane, above Oregon's McKenzie River, to the tiny cinder-block building for Sunday services.

Though heated, the church lacked indoor plumbing until the early '60s when a two-story addition brought the modern conveniences of restrooms, classrooms, and a kitchen to the building. But, I think the congregation's most prized possession was the dark, plain, upright piano.

I recall nearly losing the piano one torrential night in December 1964 when storms took out the electricity and the McKenzie River flooded its banks, threatening the properties along its path. As the water neared the building, Gordon Vance, the caretaker, came to our door to recruit help for a rescue effort. Armed with flashlights, my older brother, Dad, and my uncle immediately pulled on rain jackets and disappeared into the stormy darkness. Together they moved the heavy piano to the landing halfway up the stairs, and returned soaked and exhausted.

In seventh grade, I took piano lessons taught by my friend Jan Nash's sister. My family didn't have a piano, so I was trusted with a key to the church to practice my lessons. I found the repetitious exercises boring, and loneliness often overcame me. Through the window, I could see my siblings and friends playing in our yard. Sometimes I unlocked the door and invited the crowd in. Hide and seek or tag through the maze of rooms and hallways took priority over dumb old finger exercises.

By the middle of the '70s, the little church was in disrepair and the congregation was forced to move to the Walterville church, seven miles downriver. Keeping up appearances, Gordon Vance continued to mow the lawn and maintain the empty building. Before long, the church became a retreat center, rented for family reunions or weekend church gatherings.

I grew up, moved away from home, and barely gave the church a thought between visits. Eventually, Mrs. Austin opened a preschool in the building. Over the years, the painted handprints of perhaps sixty small children decorated the walls along the stairway, but when Gordon Vance died at age ninety, the land wasted little time growing crabgrass and dandelions, and blackberries attacked with a vengeance. Everyone could see the roof wouldn't last another rainy season. The associated church in Walterville held the deed, but the congregation wasn't wealthy and the building and land reverted to my family, the heirs of my grandmother whose land it had once been.

I'd never have dreamed I'd fall in love with my friend Jan's brother, but when Tom asked me to marry him, I didn't hesitate. Thankfully, he shared my dream of returning to Leaburg to live. Even so, neither of us had pictured living in the cinder-block church where we'd once sung hymns on Sunday mornings. But today, my husband is the one who nurtures the garden and fights blackberries to tame our little paradise.

The wood structure added on in the early '60s has been torn away, leaving only the original building, and where once a solid gray wall blocked the river view, we now sit and gaze through wide windows. The McKenzie's waters still roll west, occasionally threatening to flood, and on December 31 friends and family still come to help us ring in the New Year.

From our front room, we observe the river changing from green to dirty brown, and watch it swell with winter rain. The garden flourishes, our hair grows grayer, and we wonder what surprising twists the coming years will deliver. ༺ঌ

A Mother's Love

by Sue A. Bentley | *Ann Arbor, Michigan*

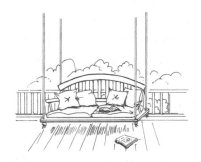

AS I DRIVE DOWN THE STREETS of my neighborhood in Ann Arbor, Michigan, I feel a sense of pride, both in my community and in its educators. If it hadn't been for my roots and the hope that sprouted here, things might have been very different in my life and in the life of my twenty-five-year-old son.

It began early on, this feeling that something was not quite right with my son, but try as I might, I couldn't put a name to it. Outwardly Sheldon was fine. He was a beautiful baby and grew to be a sweet toddler. He crawled, sat, and walked right on time. In fact, he was early at learning most things. But socially, he just didn't seem interested. Thinking his lack of social interest stemmed from being an only child, I put him into day care. But the day care provider soon noticed he was happier entertaining himself with making odd noises and repetitious activities, and that he preferred to walk around and pick up things off the floor or ground and examine them for hours. She suggested I seek medical help.

It seemed Sheldon lived in a world all of his own.

As my concerns grew, so did the labels Sheldon was given: everything from mentally retarded to schizophrenic. Uncomfortable with these labels, I decided we had to find out what the real problem was. This meant leaving my beloved hometown, but I was prepared to do whatever it would take to get my son diagnosed and helped. Together we made several trips to New York and other big cities in search of specialists, but no one there seemed to know anything more than we did. Nothing they did seemed to help, so we moved back to Ann Arbor where we were surrounded by family and friends, and continued to hope for a miracle.

In 1988 my tall, lanky ten-year-old was visited by Mr. Rothstein, the school social worker, and once again my hopes rose. But Sheldon did not respond to the questions asked of him. At that time, my son was in a classroom setting for the emotionally handi-capped. But not willing to give up hope, I was pleased when one of Sheldon's teachers, Mrs. Ramsey, took a special interest in him and his behavior patterns.

Shortly after class resumed in 1989, Mrs. Ramsey called me in for a conference. During the conference she handed me a piece of paper and asked me to read its contents to see if I thought Sheldon was not only in the wrong classroom setting, but that his diagnosis was wrong, as well. As I read, I knew immediately what I had been looking for all these years. The description on the paper was of a child with autism. I nearly wept with relief. Now that I had a name for his ailment, Sheldon could get the help he needed!

After being in the program for several years, Sheldon was once again visited by Mr. Rothstein. This time Sheldon called him by name and greeted him cheerfully. Mr. Rothstein was shocked by the changes he saw and immediately set up regular visits. During that time, he brought much love into Sheldon's life and gave him the opportunities of a lifetime. He taught Sheldon how to play chess and also introduced my quiet young man to the game of basketball.

Sheldon, who was only fourteen years old at the time, was already six feet two inches tall! Any boy that age and height would find basketball refreshingly exciting.

Another beautiful soul in Sheldon's life was Ms. Weingrot. Ms. Weingrot, a caring and able teacher, was the first to take her students—including Sheldon—to the Special Olympics. If you have never been to the Special Olympics, I can only say it is the most wonderful organization I have ever been involved in. I watched with delight as my son and his classmates developed confidence in themselves, in a way that only the Special Olympics could have accomplished for them. Here they were taught they were good at sports they formerly hadn't been able to excel at, or hadn't been given a chance to be involved in.

Sheldon is now twenty-five years old and is enrolled in art classes at Washtenaw Community College. He also started Chess Club at the college; he not only loves the game, but has a goal of becoming a Chess Master.

I feel our smaller town of Ann Arbor, filled with community spirit and pride, is what brought Sheldon out of his shell and into the real world. Without the help we found in our community, in the educators in this town, Sheldon might never have developed into the wonderful young man he is today.

And each time I drive down these streets—past the schools and academic buildings—I am filled with special thanks for the many fine and outstanding teachers in the Ann Arbor public schools. They helped pave the way for a better life for my son, and for me, and for that we will always be thankful. ⟳

The Town of Ann Arbor, Michigan

Population: 114,024

Town Facts

First incorporated: 1833

Transportation: There are various forms of transportation into and out of the city, including: air travel, Amtrak, public transit, taxi, and automobile.

Location: Ann Arbor is located in southeast Michigan, forty-five miles west of Detroit and thirty-five miles north of the Ohio border.

Places of Note: From Books to Peonies

Borders bookstore—one of the two largest book chains in the country, is headquartered in Ann Arbor.

Matthaei Botanical Gardens—the 350 acres of gardens are located on Dixboro Road, on land primarily donated by Frederick C. and Mildred Hague Matthaei.

The Ann Arbor Street Art Fair—held every summer in conjunction with the Ann Arbor Summer Art Fair, and Ann Arbor's South University Art Fair.

Nichols Arboretum—a 123-acre arboretum.

From Rock Stars to Presidents: Ann Arbor counts itself among the elite when it comes to famous names. Several rock stars, including Bob Seger, Iggy Pop, and all of the members of the group MC5, claim Ann Arbor as their hometown. Additionally, a diverse group of famous students and teachers attended the University of Michigan. Some notable names include: President Gerald Ford, near-president Thomas E. Dewey, four-time Pulitzer Prize–winning poet Robert Frost, playwright Arthur Miller, Max Gail of *Barney Miller* TV fame, comedian Gilda Radner, actor James Earl Jones, soprano Jessye Norman, and singer/superstar Madonna, as well as a long list of star athletes.

Charles Guiteau, who lived with his uncle, Ann Arbor mayor W. S. Maynard, while attending Union High School, assassinated President Garfield in 1881.

On April 12, 1955, the announcement of the Salk polio vaccine was made by **Dr. Thomas Francis,** who conducted the research in Ann Arbor for his former student Jonas Salk.

President Kennedy first announced the organization of the Peace Corps on October 12, 1960, while visiting the University of Michigan. A bronze plaque has been placed on the steps of the Michigan Union to mark the spot.

The **University of Michigan Medical Center** is the largest university medical center in the world. It is also recognized as the oldest university-owned teaching facility in the country. Its burn unit was the first in the country and is believed to be the best in the Midwest.

Astronauts at the University of Michigan: the corner of South University has been designated the "McDivitt-White Corner" in honor of the sixty-two orbits of those Gemini Astronauts; University of Michigan alumnus Jack Lousma is noted in history for his space walk; and during *Apollo 15*, James Irwin, David Scott, and Al Worden founded the "Alumni Chapter of the Moon" charter when they planted the alumni flag on the moon.

In 1902, in the first **Rose Bowl Game,** the University of Michigan football team defeated Stanford 49–0.

In 1913, Ann Arbor led all Michigan cities in the size of industrial growth, and continues to be the **fastest-growing high-tech center** in the country.

Ann Arbor has consistently been named as one of the nation's **ten best places** to live, and was tied for second place in the book *The 50 Best Places to Live and Retire in the U.S.*

Ann Arbor is the world's capital for lithography, and is known as a Tree City, USA.

Friendship Interrupted

by Shirley P. Gumert | *Kilgore, Texas*

EACH TIME I RETURN to visit Kilgore, Texas, my mind wanders back to friendships made and friendships interrupted, and I wonder if Early May is still living somewhere in Texas, or if she made it out to Los Angeles or New York City to find her singing career.

Early May, her sister Mil'red, and me. We were just girls, playing together in East Texas in the 1940s. Girls playing Swinging Statues and Run, Sheep, Run; cutting out paper dolls; playing jump rope; and sitting on a street curb to eat ice cream out of Dixie cups while we watched traffic. Checking each other's skinned knees and elbows, laughing together.

That's how I remember it. I also remember that Early May could sing, with perfect pitch and rhythm, with a memory of lyrics she'd heard only once. She could also make up songs—funny songs—to sing and act out while Mil'red and I watched and laughed. I tried to play piano while Early May sang, but while I was concentrating on reading notes, she was going right on with the melody. Mil'red could play piano "by ear" and saw no use for my music books, but she smiled when she touched the ivory keys of my piano.

◄◆►

Early May and Mil'red did not go to the library with me, or to the city swimming pool or to the movie theater. They went to a grade school some blocks away, not to the one nearby, not my school. They attended another church, not my church, and my mother told me not to go into Early May and Mil'red's house because there had once been a fire there and she was afraid someone might be careless again with a kerosene lamp or woodstove. I could go into their yard, and I could talk, politely, to their parents, Monk and Judge.

Their home was behind Mamma Elder's big old-fashioned white house, and all the land and all the oil derricks around the house belonged to the Elder family. They were good people. I think Early May and Mil'red's parents worked for Mamma Elder.

When my parents built a new home and we moved outside town, I seldom saw my two close friends. And since we were now getting into our teen years and attended separate high schools, we only waved when we saw each other downtown, or had brief conversations when we met at the grocery store.

The description of that time was "separate but equal," and eventually there came a time when our teachers admonished us to put on our best manners and have courtesy and tact throughout a special assembly by a choral group from our town's "other" high school. Whatever the teachers might have feared, we loved the performance. Early May's group gave an over-the-top, multitalented, flawless performance. I clapped and cried, "Encore!" as I heard Early May's clear, sweet voice in solo. As the performers marched out, I called her name, but she went right on by . . . chin up, eyes straight ahead.

Later, I heard that Early May was offered a scholarship to college to study music but that she chose not to go. Sometime after that, I met her in the grocery and held her first child, laughed with her at the sight of his first teeth. I saw her again a few years later, with several children, and she said she lived in Dallas. When I asked her if she was still singing, she shrugged. I asked if Mil'red had a piano, and I was saddened by the answer.

As years pass, the memory of Early May drifts into and out of my consciousness. Recently, I was waiting my turn in a doctor's office. It was a cold day. A bundled-up woman came in, stepping quickly and swinging her walking cane as though it were a baton. She exclaimed about the weather, and there was music in each word she spoke. She sat opposite me, and we talked. We found things to laugh about. I wish I'd asked her name. I felt as though I'd met a friend. There we sat and laughed together for a few minutes, two aging Texas women, one black, one white.

Would we be friends today, Early May and me? . . . I wonder.

Over all these years, I've wanted her to be Ruby Dee, Leontyne Price, Maya Angelou, Debbie Allen. Did she wish for me a Pulitzer Prize, a Newbery Award, a shelf full of books with my name listed as author? How might we have cheered for each other through our lives? How much laughter have we missed?

I don't remember talking about our dreams or our talents or the color of our skin when we were children. Early May just sang, and I'll never find the right words to tell the true joy of hearing it. ও

Sleeping at the Foot of the Bed

by Mary Ralph Bradley | *Ralph Hollow, Tennessee*

GROWING UP, I OFTEN LISTENED to a country song called "Sleeping at the Foot of the Bed," by Little Jimmy Dickens. In that song he sings about having to "take an old cold tater and wait" because "taters never did taste good with chicken on the plate."

Did Little Jimmy Dickens actually experience those delightful doings? I know not. But as a child growing up in Ralph Hollow, Tennessee, I did.

Growing up with a dad, a mom, eight siblings, and a grandma always around the table, as well as wayfaring strangers staying overnight—well, you can imagine how I fared. When no chicken was left, my mother's potatoes still tasted pretty good to a hungry youngster!

We were a large family, but we really never wanted for anything, and I still resent probing questions such as, "How do your parents take care of all nine of you?" Dad and Mom were so inventive and intelligent that we had no idea we were poor. Though we wore hand-me-down clothes, we held our heads high. We were told we were as good as the next person. To our parents, it was especially important that we all get an education—something many of our neighbors did not do.

Daddy, a carpenter in a nearby town, and Mama, a farmer, carpenter, cook, housekeeper, disciplinarian, and hostess, were the most gracious of all parents. In the '30s, when Dad saw someone walking, he offered them a ride, usually bringing the individual home with him for supper. If the person spent the night, my sister and I had to slip into bed with two other sisters or sleep on the floor at the foot of the bed.

"Why," I asked my mom one day, "do we have to take in every stranger who comes along? Uncle Frank and Aunt Bertha never let anyone spend the night." As I recall, Mom had little time for foolish questions and all I got was a stern glance.

I remember old Mrs. Bush and her young, frail grandson who came home with Daddy one evening. They needed to get to Gainesboro, sixty miles away, for the funeral of her son the next day.

"Where will they get the money to ride the bus?" queried my brother, L. D.

"You'll see," replied Daddy.

After supper Daddy said, "Come on, children. Go with me up the road." The road was a narrow, unpaved strip known as Long Hollow Pike that ran between two hills from Goodlettsville to Shackle Island.

Dad stopped at the first house. "All right, you two," he said, looking at me and my brother, "go in there and tell Uncle Frank we need some money for these people." In we went, never doubting our success. Uncle Frank had nothing, but turned to bachelor brother Uncle Tom, who always had money. We thanked Uncle Tom and ran back to the car with two quarters.

L. D. was sent out at the next house and also came back with two quarters. I was tickled that I got to go to the next house because Mr. Green, one of my favorite people, lived there and ran a sorghum mill. He must have liked me, too, because I came back to the car with a whole dollar!

Two or three more stops and our bounty had risen to $4.75, plenty for our travelers. The next morning, after they were fed a good breakfast, Dad took them to the bus station before heading to his carpenter shop.

One of my favorite visitors was Mr. Joe Acree, who was with us often. In those days, salesmen rode buses to towns and walked to the country stores to take orders. Mr. Joe was always neatly dressed—blue serge suit, white shirt, and a tie. One particular visit lingers in my mind as an example of how serious my mother took hospitality.

"Now, you children be good tonight," said Mother. "Mr. Acree will be eating with us."

We quickly nodded. With only one guest, we could all still sit at the table for a meal. At dinnertime, L. D. was on my left and Mr. Joe on my right, at the head of the table. Just as I raised a glass of buttermilk to my lips, L. D. pinched my leg. You can imagine my horror to see all those white spots spray across Mr. Joe's suit, but it was not half as much as the horror I next felt. With the swish of her left hand, Mama struck me, just as the cloth in her right hand rapidly wiped the milk from our startled guest's suit. That was the only slap I ever received from my mother, but that was enough to cure L. D. and me of horseplay at the table for good.

Besides working at his carpenter shop and writing a weekly newspaper column, Dad grew fruits and vegetables on the hill behind our house. Most summer nights we followed him to the top of the hill where he removed his hat and knelt down to pray in thanks for his bounty. Mama helped to make extra money, as well. She raised chickens, sheep, cows, and hogs. We actually ate better than most of our neighbors because my parents were so industrious and taught each of us a strong work ethic.

Today when I visit my sister who lives in our childhood home, I see the old barn still standing firm, the hen house lacking chickens but filled with nostalgia. I recall our experiences in the '30s and know they molded me into a better person. Those days taught me tolerance and understanding. I love to help the sick, cook for friends, and remember all the important lessons I learned from great parents. I am now eighty years of age, work every day in a law office, run my fifty-acre farm, and take part in our town's many activities. The Lord blesses me more each day with good health, wonderful children, and fantastic friends, but memories of home and Ralph Hollow are the foundation of all that I am. ꩜

State Route 149

by Roberta Rhodes | *North English, Iowa*

"For Adoption." That's what the sign said.

We had exited I-80 about a hundred miles east of Des Moines and were driving south through some of the richest farmland in the world: south, on State Route 149, through Williamsburg, and Parnell. That's where I saw the sign, just outside Parnell. It read: "This Highway for Adoption."

I'd like that. I'd like to adopt this highway, this little handful of Iowa right here, where the grassy meadow falls away to that clump of trees—mulberries, box elders, elms—standing so close together it's hard to see the creek at their base, but I know it's there. It's a restful creek, a quiet creek. I wonder, upstream, did it water cattle and farmers and their families? And did it feel the slipping, squishing of little bare feet cooling off after a day in the fields? No matter, it now meanders placidly around the feet of a clump of trees on a grassy meadow near Iowa State Route 149.

I think I would choose this piece of highway because my heart chooses this piece of Iowa. As children, we visited my grandfather's farm in North English, a few miles from here. Very late one summer night our car—was it the '36 Pontiac?—got hopelessly stuck in the mud of the county line road just at the bottom of the hill from Grandpa's. There was nothing to do but remove our shoes and socks, get out of the car, and trudge our way up the road through the country dark to the farmhouse on foot. And as we slogged our way through the mud, the plaintive voice of my little brother observed, "Grandpa's sidewalks sure are slippery." The next morning Grandpa hitched up a team of horses and pulled our car out.

Daddy and Mother both grew up in rural Iowa, so I feel a kind of *you-can-go-home-again* longing for a little spot like this. During their childhood years on the farm, from roughly 1908 through the 1920s, things were pretty much as they had been for centuries. That was before the tractor, electricity, and indoor plumbing. Mother remembers that they grew their own breakfast: bacon, eggs, butter, cream, even sorghum molasses for the pancakes. And when they had company coming to dinner, they killed, scalded, plucked, cut up, and cooked a chicken; dug some potatoes; picked some beans, tomatoes, and lettuce. They made a pie crust from lard they're rendered themselves, and filled it with gooseberries they'd picked. In those days, Iowa farmers were nearly self-sustaining. Mother's parents raised everything they needed, except sugar and coffee. And their stability was the stuff America was made of, so, yes, I'd like a piece of that.

Now, I know when signs speak of adopting a highway they mean pick up the trash and keep the countryside clean. In fact, every year hundreds of groups have taken on thousands of miles of highway, and done so happily in exchange for getting their names on the sign. But I don't want my name on a sign. All I want is something tucked away in my memory: a soothing soulscape to slip into when I'm overwhelmed by sidewalk and paving. I want a grassy meadow that falls away to a clump of trees beside a quiet creek whose waters murmur, "Welcome home."

There is such a place and it calls to me, from just off Iowa State Route 149.

Rotary Club Pianist

by Lanita Bradley Boyd | *Portland, Tennessee*

SLIPPING OUT OF CHEMISTRY CLASS, I quickly walked to the front door of the school. As usual, Mitchell Moore was waiting to escort me to the weekly meeting of the Portland Rotary Club. Mr. Mitchell (so-called out of courtesy) stood beside his car, a car that was almost as aged as he, and gallantly opened the door for me.

Greeting me warmly, he shuffled around to the driver's side of the car. A bit shriveled with age, he peered over the steering wheel as he slowly pulled away from the curb. Fortunately, all of Portland moved rather slowly in 1962, so Mr. Mitchell's methodical driving caused little concern.

We traveled the few blocks to the Chandler building, passed Chandler Dry Goods on the first floor, and climbed the oiled stairs to the room where the Rotarians were assembled. Most weeks I was the only female present, and the men were incredibly kind and appreciative. Occasionally they would have a special day when their wives were invited, and I was always amused at how they referred to the women as "Rotary-Anns."

As soon as we arrived, the meeting began. It was called to order and we all stood for the Pledge of Allegiance. Then I sat at the piano and played from *All America Sings* as they sang "America the Beautiful," "My Country 'Tis of Thee," or "The Star-Spangled Banner." We had a prayer, usually by a minister who was invited for that purpose, before we ate.

Our lunch was catered by a couple of local women who cooked it in their kitchen and brought it to the meeting hall, but at the time we never used the word "catered." The president would simply say, "We're so grateful to Wanda and Lenora for fixing us this delicious dinner," and everyone would applaud while Wanda and Lenora blushed. The program would begin while we were eating because the men were conscientious about keeping it to the hour that most people had for lunch.

I have no idea what the topics were. I'm not sure I could have told you even then. I was simply aware that no matter where I looked, there was an old man looking at me and smiling.

If there was any of the hour left after the speaker had finished, I would be asked to play again. They would choose songs such as "Rose of Tralee" or "I'll Take You Home Again, Kathleen" and really belt them out. I'm sure the low ceilings of the room increased the volume of their voices, but I was always grateful they sang so boisterously because it covered up any mistakes I made. Since I never knew what they might request, I made no pretense of practicing for the event. The president would end by thanking me, always saying something flowery about how my presence was "like a breath of fresh air."

Over the years, I was one in a long line of senior girls who were chosen to play for the Rotary Club. I didn't fool myself into thinking it was because of my expert playing. I suspected that it had something to do with my having a convenient lunch schedule or having been one of Mr. Mitchell's wife's favorite students.

After we got back in the car, Mr. Mitchell would ceremoniously hand me two one-dollar bills and say, "Thank you for doing such a wonderful job of playing for us, Lanita. I don't know what we'd do without you."

Then he would drive me back to school, insisting that I wait until he walked around the car to open the door for me. I felt like a princess alighting from her carriage. Now, years later, each time I return to visit Portland and see the old high school, long since replaced by a more modern facility, I recall how Mr. Mitchell and his associates made an insignificant small-town girl feel immensely treasured. ⟨⟩

Single Vision

by Lad Moore | *Marshall, Texas*

SHAKESPEARE WROTE: "The sun with one eye vieweth all the world."
I don't know the context in which he wrote it, but it always reminded
me of me. My life is a scrapbook of rare prints—an odd postcard
collection that skipped all of the ordinary destinations. I cherish
them all.

My parents divorced when I was six months old. I don't
remember my mother. I studied her likeness in some photos my
grandmother saved, and told friends she was Cherokee Indian. All
the kids believed Cherokee was an ancestry to brag about. Maybe
my lying was a way to salvage some pride about her leaving me. It
was good she had high cheekbones and dark skin. I think my friends
believed me.

My father seemed forever absent, following his dream in the
uniform of a soldier of fortune. In my favorite photo of him, he is
posed in front of the Great Pyramids, arms clasped behind his back,
wearing khakis—the kind with excessive pockets. I can almost feel
the heat and see the dust swirling around him. The photo symbol-
ized the notion of things far away: the image I always held of him.

During his overseas flying missions, I stayed with my grand-mother in a modest frame home in Marshall, Texas, a town best remembered for its time as temporary capital of the state of Missouri during the Civil War. Marshall has a rich history, notable architectural treasures, and boasts the nearby childhood home of Lady Bird Johnson.

I called my grandmother Mommie Moore. I always used both names. It seemed formal to say it that way, but it invoked the deep and reverent respect I held for her. Our time together in the little house on George Gregg Street was a hallmark of all things predictable and safe.

My quiet East Texas lifestyle was interrupted periodically when my father sent for me. The times I spent with him were like a pinball game, buffeting around from stop to stop. We seemed to follow no maps and never put down roots. I attended ten different schools, including one year aboard a freighter, sailing the ports from New York to Java. A tutor traveled with me, teaching from a correspondence school curriculum.

The pauses between our overseas posts were always welcome rest stops. I looked forward to them because it meant returning to East Texas. There, I could count on things being simple, unhurried. I could just be a boy. I loved the feel of the red clay squishing between my toes on rainy days. My soul found reassurance in the soft whisper of the pine needles in the morning breeze.

A few miles down Old Stagecoach Road lay sprawling Caddo Lake. Part swamp, part river, it meandered its way well into Louisiana. It had that classic "river rat" look—rough shanties on stilts and Spanish moss tapestries streaming from cypress limbs. The dark bayous and heavy thickets were surrounded by folklore and legend—plenty of fodder for a young boy's imagination. Old maps listed such places as Horse Island, Hog Wallow, Turtle Shell, and Whangdoodle Pass. There was a lantern-glow tale to go with every name.

The caramel-colored waters of the Big Cypress River always brought memories of Huck Finn's adventures to the surface. The river was where I learned the art of frog-grabbing with a flashlight. I also took some lessons from the River Skiff Bible—how alligator eyes glow red at night, and how water moccasins often drape themselves on tree branches, poised to drop their mushy plumpness into one's boat.

My friends and I often enjoyed the bounty of the lake. The menu was usually catfish and frog legs, fried crispy brown under the canopy of a giant live oak called Big Top. After a hearty meal washed down with red soda pop, we lay on the soft grass and searched for four-leaf clovers—but only if within arm's reach.

My father died just after my fourteenth birthday. His life was hurried, like his death at age forty-one. I remember him telling me once that he would probably die in his airplane, in a steep nosedive into some rice paddy somewhere. Instead, he died of self-inflicted wounds—the slow poison of alcohol. It was a powerful moral lesson for me.

The next few years rushed by. I finished high school with honors, got my college degree, married, and began my own family. I entered the corporate world and began my climb up the rungs of business success. In my thirty-three-year career, my duty stations were mostly fast-track cities and overstuffed boardrooms. I often stared out fiftieth-floor windows and thought about East Texas, but my career kept me far from there.

When at last I began to consider retirement, location was an open catalog of choice. With no encumbrances and widely scattered children, I could have gone anywhere. Several Florida destinations made the top ten, as did the golfing paradises around Hilton Head, South Carolina. Australia even made the must-see list. Marshall, Texas, wouldn't have made the list at all, if I hadn't felt that gentle tug from inside that said, "Come home."

Maybe it was the historic brick streets or the echoes of the freight trains under the viaduct. Or maybe it was just the fond recollections of Mommie Moore and the barefoot summers of East Texas. After cursory consideration, we set aside the slick retirement brochures. We traded them for the mysteries of Caddo Lake, the smell of burning magnolia leaves on a fall afternoon, and Marshall's annual Fire Ant Festival. It was a chance to reconnect with our roots, and to restore relationships with childhood friends who spun off into orbit like us, but returned safely to the launch site.

In the end, my "one eye in the sun" simply looked over my shoulder. In the distance rose the seven red-clay hills of Marshall, Texas. But what it really saw was the inseparable link between heart and home. ᠔

The Power of Oma's Popcorn

by Garnet Hunt White | *Doniphan, Ripley County, Missouri*

AFTER I RETURNED to my hometown to live, I learned my mother's popcorn—found only at Hunt Theatre in the Ozark town of Doniphan, in Ripley County, Missouri—had a great influence on the customers.

Because my husband, Glenn, traveled on his job and Doniphan was about the center of his territory, we decided to move back to our hometown after being gone for eighteen years. When Glenn was on the road, I worked in my parents' movie theater.

I learned a lot in that theater.

For instance, when logging and lumber groups got off work and came straight to the movie asking for five big sacks of popcorn and two large sodas, I realized they hadn't eaten anything else all day. I also learned that my father, Garrett Hunt, had a head for business and knew how to use it. He gave truck drivers free passes to the movies if they hauled loads of customers to the theater on their flatbed trucks.

My father had a ticket-selling strategy: never turn away customers. Find seats. My main job was locating seats for the late arrivals.

On December 18 and 19, 1952, Gary Cooper and Grace Kelly starred in *High Noon.* The theater seats filled quickly. About fifteen minutes into the movie, Rett and Ella Markson came in and announced they'd buy tickets if they could get good seats.

"Oma or Garnet," my father hollered. "Find them good seats."

I mumbled under my breath, "Impossible to find seats tonight." Then, like a good usher, I went up and down every aisle twice, even though I knew there were no good seats left in the house. As I passed the center walkway, I noticed the Deaton family. They were a family of meager income. Though they only bought two adult tickets and two children's tickets, they occupied eight seats. Thinking quickly, I asked, "Mrs. Deaton, if Mother gave Bart and Tiff two big sacks of corn, would they give up their seats and go to the front?"

The boys yelled, "Yes!" Mrs. Deaton and I laughed as they jumped from their seats and rushed to get Mother's popcorn.

As I ushered Rett and Ella to the seats, Ella asked, "How did you find such good seats?"

"It wasn't easy," I replied as I saw two towheaded boys munching popcorn on their way to the front.

Though Hunt Theatre tickets cost only ten and thirty-five cents, my parents gave away many free tickets and free popcorn to people who couldn't afford them. Those who just got out of the hospital or were involved in an accident rated free passes, too.

That particular night, after the movie ended, Mother gave Bart an additional eight bags of leftover corn for his brothers, sister, and their parents. Bart quickly passed them out and thanked her with a wide smile on his face.

The next Saturday night, when the Deaton family arrived at the movies, Bart leaned on the ticket desk and with a serious look on his face addressed my father. "Garrett, if you need seats tonight, me and Tiff will let you have our seats for popcorn."

"Thank you, Bart," Garrett answered. "We'll keep you in mind. Better tell Oma and Garnet what you'll do."

Bart rushed to Mother and me at the popcorn machine. "Me and Tiff will give up our seats tonight for popcorn."

"We'll remember that," we told him.

During the show that night when I ushered customers past Bart, he leaned far out into the aisle to ask, "Do you need mine and Tiff's seats?" As it turned out, the theater filled up quickly and it wasn't long before I ended up buying their seats.

The following Tuesday night the Deatons came to the movie again, and though Hunt Theatre never had a full house midweek, Bart kept asking, "Need our seats?"

On Saturday night, December 26, Hunt Theatre had a packed house. Wise Bart observed the crowd and ran to the lobby yelling for my father. Pop, thinking something terrible had happened, jumped up from his chair.

"What's wrong, Bart?" he asked.

"Garrett!" Bart said, grabbing Pop's hand. "If you need seats, I'll take my little brothers down to the front. That's four seats you can have if you'll give us popcorn."

Pop suppressed the smile he always wore when he talked to Bart about his entrepreneurial skills. Putting his hand on the boy's head, he said, "Bart, you're a real trader. You'll do alright when you grow up."

That night Bart managed to sell all four seats. ∾

Sugar Cookies and Quilts

by Betty Downs | *Clyde, North Dakota*

IF MY HOUSE CAUGHT ON FIRE, or the wind tore the roof off, one of the things I would want to rescue would be Mamma's quilt. The quilt hangs on my bedroom wall so I can see it every day. It centers me as I walk past the history it represents. It offers me a slice of my childhood, which was spent on a wheat farm near Clyde, North Dakota. It gives me the memory of my mother at a time in her life when she was young, happy, and vibrant.

When she was diagnosed with terminal cancer, I returned home to spend as much time with her as possible. After Mamma's death, the thought of her last days haunted me—that is, until we opened the trunk that held her treasures.

"Oh, look!" I cried, spying the quilt down at the bottom. Lifting it from its dark hiding place, I realized it was wrapped around memories of long ago.

Pictures jumped into my mind as my fingers touched the long bars of pink, the round, colorful circles with black embroidery stitches. All of a sudden, I remembered walking with Mother the mile or so to Aunt Mary's house.

◄o►

Aunt Mary and Uncle Pete lived on the old Hyde place, in a little white bungalow at the top of a hill. Their house was part of the magical five-year-old world I had lived in. Since they had no children of their own, whenever I was a visitor, I was made to feel very special. Sweet sugar cookies were always waiting for me.

Holding the quilt, I closed my eyes, and was five years old again sitting on Aunt Mary's linoleum-covered living room floor, playing with little snippets of cloth. Triangles, circles, and tiny strips of pink, blue, green, yellow, and orange material floated to the floor as I sat under the table constructing my own designs. Mother and Aunt Mary stood above me, bending over the intricate pattern that became the very quilt I now hold. I smiled as Mamma's face once again became young, soft, and gently beautiful.

Those two happy, laughing ladies patiently stitched, by hand, the pieces of colorful cotton that made up the design in the quilting frame. It was a quilt like no other, a design resulting from Aunt Mary's perfectionism, and Mother's imagination. Mother was the queen of "making do," and Aunt Mary, the perfectionist, could clean chickens all day and still look like she stepped out of a fashion magazine. Together, they were a dynamic duo.

Mother was very artistic, but so down-to-earth her artistry always resulted in something that could be used in a commonsense way. She sewed all my clothes. The big box sent yearly all the way from Illinois, where rich Aunt Clara lived, contained fashionable dresses and hardly worn coats that Mother ripped up and reconstructed into wearable clothing for me. I was eleven years old before I wore a dress that Mother hadn't sewn from bleached flour sacks, or pieces of someone else's clothing.

As I held the quilt tightly in my arms and returned to the present, I realized this quilt was an exception; it was made from new material. Soft cotton polyester was unheard of in 1933 when this quilt was pieced together, but the coarse cotton was now soft due to age.

This morning, as I hold the precious piece of cloth to my cheek, the simplicity of it is a reminder of a time in my life when colorful scraps of material and sugar cookies were all that was needed for an entertaining afternoon. The colors remind me of the laughter and joy that was shared on that summer's day. The delicate stitching throughout the quilt gives me a sense of perfect, yet commonsense, order.

Putting the quilt down, I remember that Hallie, my four-year-old granddaughter, is coming to visit today. Smiling, I run my fingertips across the colorful squares. Perhaps it was time Hallie and I stirred up some cookies and relived history. ᴖ

The Town of
Clyde, North Dakota

Population:
Varies slightly from four in the off-season
to five during the peak season.

History

The Tallman Investment Company of Willmar, Minnesota, laid out the town of Clyde on state land in 1905, the same year the railroad reached the area. To please the many Scottish settlers in the region, the town was named Clyde, after a town in Scotland.

In November 1905, the post office was established, and other businesses followed suit, including: a mercantile, a general store, a hardware store, a drugstore, a blacksmith, two lumber companies, a pool hall, and a livery stable. In later years, more shops opened. Before long a car dealership, a jewelry store, a bank, and a hotel were added to the downtown district.

In 1906, the first school was opened, followed in 1907 by a two-room school. The Catholic and Methodist churches were built shortly after the town was founded.

The Clyde community peaked in the 1920s, with 275 residents, but with the onslaught of a serious drought in the 1930s, coupled with the Great Depression, the population began to diminish. By 1940, it had declined to 80 residents, and remained there until the 1960s. Today, Clyde's population is at an all-time low. Only three families and three businesses remain within the community, but all appear happy to be there. ✑

Town Facts

First incorporated: The community of Clyde was never incorporated as a town—it remains a part of Bruce Township, within Cavalier County.

Transportation: In the early days, travel was by horse and buggy, but as the railroad reached town, travel by rail became popular.

Location: Clyde is located in a fertile farming area, thirty miles from three towns that have a population of about 2,000 each—Langdon, Cando, and Rolla. One of the reasons for Clyde's population decline may have been because it was settled just fifteen miles from the Canadian border, on a major highway—it was just so easy for people to get out of town.

Noteworthy Facts

Scottish families came to the area on immigrant trains.

The word *Clyde* is the shortened form of *Cledwyn*, which is the name of a major Scottish river.

At one time, the male residents of Clyde had an active Knights of Pythias Lodge, which was the largest in all of North Dakota, with more than 150 members.

One evening, residents left their fields and retired for the night, and woke eight hours later to a drastically changed world . . . during the course of the night, grasshoppers had completely devoured everything in sight for as far as the eye could see.

Where I Belong

by Rhoda Novak | *Brownsville, Pennsylvania*

I WAS NINETEEN, EXCITED TO BE STUDYING physics at Carnegie Mellon University, but more excited that my lab partner, John, had invited me to his home to meet his parents. We left school and drove down Route 40 to Brownsville, a small coal-mining town southeast of Pittsburgh. I gripped my hands in my lap as we went up a steep, pebbled drive high above the river. It wasn't the drive that had my stomach all tied up in knots, it was the uncertainty of whether John's parents would like me or not. I gulped as he stopped at the second house in a row of about a dozen small homes.

John's mother came out onto the porch as our car pulled up, her heavy coat and wool scarf hiding all but the gray braids wrapped around her head and her welcoming smile. "You'll catch your death of cold—what with the wind and all," she said as she hugged John. "Come on in." She cast a gentle eye my way. "You must be Rhoda."

"Pleased to meet you, Mrs. Novak," I replied.

"Call me Momma," she said, taking my arm. "Let me introduce you to Poppa."

We entered the family room where a small black-and-white television blared out the news. John's father, ensconced in the oversized brown easy chair, placed his Meerschaum pipe on the TV tray and stood up, arms outstretched. He was a lean, vibrant man with thinning black hair that was beginning to gray around the temples. Under his black-framed glasses, intense blue eyes peered into mine, and then he smiled.

"I've been looking forward to meeting you, Rhoda," he said, holding out his hand. "Our daughter is also a physicist. Bet the teachers give you a hard time."

I laughed as he looked deeply into my eyes in a soul-searching gaze. After a moment, he turned and said, "Welcome home, Son."

Outside the storm swirled, but inside all was warm and cozy. Momma took my coat and walked us into the kitchen, keeping the conversation going despite my suddenly tongue-tied disposition. She smiled and nodded her head at her son. "I've been waiting to set eyes on you, Rhoda. John says you're special."

Embarrassed, I looked about the warm kitchen. It smelled of chicken soup, cinnamon, and Five Brothers tobacco. The pantry doors bulged with staples—Crisco, sugar, and Quaker oats—but I was surprised there were no vegetables.

"You should see the shelves in the basement," John said, reading my mind. "Momma grows and cans all our vegetables."

"That's a lot of work," I replied, looking at Momma with a new sense of wonderment.

"Poppa's allergic to preservatives and anyway store-bought cans don't taste good," she said with a wave of her hand.

John smiled. "Don't let her be modest. They cultivate an acre with my uncles at Grandpa's farm."

Momma immediately shushed her son. "Now Johnny, if you don't have nothing better to do than to flap your mouth, go talk to

Poppa. He's been waiting all day," she said, pushing him out of the kitchen.

Suddenly alone with this vivacious woman, I felt overwhelmed. To hide my anxiety, I walked over to the table and sat down. It was one of those tables from the '50s, yellow Formica and chrome. Though a small square tablecloth with crocheted edges was laid across the center of the table, much of the surface was exposed. The tabletop had so many scratches on it that if I closed my eyes, I knew I would see John sitting there doing his homework, his father paying the bills, and their family and friends munching nut rolls.

Sitting on the table was a green salad bowl filled with fresh picked lettuce, tomatoes, radishes, and onions sliced paper thin. A stainless steel thermos with piping hot coffee sat next to an oversized, chipped coffee mug labeled *Daddy*. It was within arm's reach of the worn rocking chair that John had said his father used every morning.

My eyes fell on Momma as she opened the old electric oven and checked the temperature with her hand, counting the seconds before she had to pull it away from the heat. Smiling, she said, "Just perfect," and put in the tin tray with spirals of cinnamon rolls. "You'ns hungry?" Addressing the doorway that led back to the room John and his father sat in, Momma hollered, "Just wait a speck and supper will be on."

After that, Momma pulled the chicken out of the pot and put it on the cutting board. "No sense waiting for the menfolk to help. They're talking up a storm."

In a moment, we were working together in the kitchen as if we had always done so. As I cut the chicken into thick, juicy slices, she set it on an orange serving plate. She added salt and pepper then spooned rich, golden broth into different colored bowls. "Supper's ready. Won't be no good if it gets cold," she called.

When John and Poppa came to the table, she asked, "How you doing, Johnny? College keeping you busy?"

"Yeah, Momma," John said as he looked at me. "Glad I've got such a good lab partner."

Blushing, I served the soup as Momma put the rolls on the table. Momma nodded at me. "You got a good girl here," she said.

"I like her myself," John answered teasingly as he touched my arm. "Think I'll marry her."

"I could use another daughter," Momma said as she enveloped me in her arms. Relief that I had been accepted rolled over me and I closed my eyes, trying not to cry. It had been so long since my own mother had held me like that, and Momma's hug felt so much like my mother's, that I couldn't help sniffling back tears. And when she whispered, "Welcome home," I couldn't help but think that was exactly what I had done. I had come home. ❧

Passing Strangers

by Joyce Stark | *Weed, California*

LIKE MOST THINGS IN LIFE, sometimes it's the passing stranger who immediately picks up the sense of history or the warmth of a community. My husband and I have been fortunate enough to be *passing strangers* and to drop in on small-town America for a good number of years now.

When we first came home from a vacation and spoke to friends in Scotland about how the best bits of our vacation were spent in small-town America, they hadn't a clue what we were talking about. Their idea of the United States was New York, San Francisco, or Chicago, so our stories were intriguing to them, especially about one particular small town.

As we drove north through California, headed toward Oregon, we just had to stop in a town by the name of Weed. What we found there was so typical of small-town America that it will live with me forever. We discovered a town founded by a man whose name had been Mr. Weed. According to the locals, Mr. Weed had built a thriving community around the lumber industry. Pictures hung on the local museum walls showing hundreds and hundreds of people working in the timber yards around Weed. But as with many small towns, when the big business in the area—in this case the lumber business—was bought, dismantled, and moved elsewhere, Weed began to suffer. Many of the businesses closed down; it was hard for youngsters to find jobs to stay in the area.

We were delighted that the townsfolk took the time to tell us how they remembered Weed in its busy days. It seemed everyone had a relative, often many relatives, who were involved in the lumber business.

Oddly, our motel was virtually full. Locals explained it away by telling us that people are drawn by the strange name and the fact that Weed lies close to the base of the beautiful Mount Shasta. Everyone we met seemed happy. This was a town of joy. Negativity was absent, and every visitor was welcomed. Everyone said "Good morning" or offered strangers help when it came to getting to know the town or choosing the best route to take on their journey when it was time to leave Weed behind. I couldn't help thinking that it was the people as much as the little town's history and beautiful surroundings that brought people back to it.

Though today's Main Street is pretty quiet in Weed, the people are philosophical, like small-town folks the world over. The subject causing the most debate when we were there wasn't the war abroad or the latest political issue, it was the fact that someone outside town had built a house with three garages.

"Who needs three garages?" one man asked.

"Well, I probably would have them, if I could afford them," another one said.

"You only have one tractor—you would fill the other two with rubbish!" The first man replied.

Those enjoying breakfast in the little diner listened to the conversation with a smile on their faces. I felt they would go about their day thinking about the rights and wrongs of three garages rather than anything else, and somehow I found that idea pleasant and not at all out of character.

Things are more laid back in small-town America.

For instance, early one morning I met a young man in his twenties sitting outside a shop on Main Street carving a beautiful deer from a piece of wood, wearing that slow smile small towners tend to have cornered. His story was simple, yet it struck a chord deep down inside of me.

As he spoke, his hands continued working. "My grandfather and my father worked either in the forests or in the lumber yards. I always intended to follow their example, but the lumber business moved on. I found I had a gift for anything artistic, like painting, sculpture, and this. . . ." He smiled. "I rarely paint or do anything but carve these wooden animals." Shrugging his shoulders, he said, "I suppose wood is in my blood."

It was obvious he was never going to be rich and yet everyone passing waved and spoke to him. As I watched, I suddenly realized I was wrong about his wealth. This young man was rich, indeed. That morning I felt as if the whole town was part of a very large family, a family that had suffered and yet held together.

In the restaurant and in the bar, if one person was talking to us, six more joined in. Quite often, they squabbled over telling us the best things to see in the area. Sometimes we just sat back and relaxed as the argument spread, but everyone ended up smiling in the end.

It wasn't just that every one of them knew everyone else, it was that they also cared about each other. Everywhere you went you heard comments such as, "Where have you been?" "How did your visit to your cousin's go?" "Have you seen George recently, maybe we should call in and check if he is okay?"

The pace of life in small towns might be slow, but the strength of character is strong. It's that natural caring that brings us back to small-town America time and time again. ❧

The Bricks of Fort Scott

by Nancy Gustafson | *Fort Scott, Kansas*

I PARK MY CAR ON MAIN STREET and stare intently at a house I hardly recognize. It is a shambles. Its murky gray paint and blue trim are as smeared and faded as a watercolor painting left in the rain. Bricks are loose in the chimney and the turret above the tiny front porch is sagging. The shutters present a toothless sneer, and so many shingles are missing that there must be roof leaks. The house is weeping, and so am I.

Stepping out of my car onto the native-brick street, I crouch down and run my finger along the name embedded in a brick: Fort Scott. Every brick in the street is embedded with the name of the town. Like Dorothy, who wandered lost in Oz and finally found her way home, I'm back in Kansas.

As I straighten, I imagine the house the way it looked when my Great Aunt Marie Gunsaullus lived in it. Shiplap boards painted bright white with dark green trim signaled a welcome to family and friends. Daylilies and ferns bent and bowed in the flowerbeds around the sturdy foundation, and an intricate wicker swing beckoned from the porch. My eyes travel to an ancient pear tree growing in the side yard, and I find myself hoping it is the same tree I climbed more than fifty years ago.

Aunt Marie was born in 1886, forty-four years after Fort Scott was established by the Army to keep peace along the Permanent Indian Frontier, and five years after Kansas entered the Union as a free state. She began her teaching career in Maple Grove, Kansas, in 1907, earning $30 per month, and ended it in Fort Scott in 1952 when she retired. One year before her death at ninety-five years of age, she was named to the Kansas Retired Teachers Hall of Fame, in Dodge City. As she had requested, the old school bell from Maple Grove was rung in her memory.

I step quickly to the curb when I hear car tires thumping on the brick street behind me, and am transported back to one of my most treasured memories—an excursion with Aunt Marie in her Model T Ford. On that particular day our errand took us to Cousin Gladys's dairy farm to get milk and cream. As if it were yesterday, I can see Aunt Marie donning her summer motoring hat, with its broad straw brim and black band, while I grabbed the glass milk bottles. Bending over stiffly, she gave the Model T a couple of cranks and we were off.

Intent upon her destination, and seemingly unconcerned about other cars on the road, Aunt Marie aimed the Model T directly down the middle of the street, and we clipped along at fifteen miles an hour. Soon we were out of town, chugging down a farm-to-market road, hitting every pothole and raising a cloud of dust. When I hit my head on the ceiling as we rumbled over a wooden bridge, Aunt Marie pulled me close to her and with a flinty expression cautioned, "Slow down, Sister!"

As usual, the Model T announced our arrival with a coughing fit before shutting down, and Cousin Gladys immediately waddled out to greet us. "Come on in and have some gingerbread," she hollered. "I'm about to take it out of the oven." I smiled like the

Cheshire cat. Nothing could compare with the comfort of her country kitchen, drenched in the delicious aromas of coffee, molasses, and cinnamon. After I was stuffed with warm gingerbread, and a milk moustache decorated my upper lip, we took our milk and cream and retraced our route.

But that was all a very long time ago.

I cross the street and lay my hand on the stone wall that keeps the front yard from falling onto the sidewalk. Wistfully, I note that the wall is not as high as I had once thought. The house is crumbling and Aunt Marie is gone.

As I walk solemnly to my car, I take in the neighborhood with one last sweeping glance and a smile touches my face. Buildings may crumble, but memories of all I loved are embedded in my mind as deeply as the name Fort Scott is embedded in each brick beneath my feet. ∿

Love at First Sight

by Sandy Williams Driver | *Albertville, Alabama*

DALTON WILLIAMS RETURNED to the United States in 1945 with a promotion to Private First Class and a different look in his royal blue eyes. He bore little resemblance to the naive farm lad who had bravely signed his name on an enlistment form the year before.

The terrors of the jungle left permanent marks on many of the soldiers who fought in Burma, including quiet, twenty-one-year-old Dalton. After being awarded an honorable discharge from the Army, he wanted only one thing: to go home. He had seen enough of big cities and crowded ships during his tour of duty in the Asiatic Pacific and longed for the peaceful way of life in his small, rural hometown of Albertville, high atop Sand Mountain in northern Alabama.

Dalton was welcomed back to civilian life with open arms. He walked proudly around town, stopping often to chat with old friends or receive a pat on the back and a handshake from folks for his faithful service, and painful sacrifices, to his country.

Making his way toward the general store one Saturday morning, he heard his sister Jewell call his name. When he looked up, he saw Jewell standing beside a rickety wagon that held the most beautiful girl he had ever seen. Intrigued, he quickly joined them, wasting no time in introducing himself to the lovely stranger.

As Ilene watched the handsome young man, she was thankful she'd come along that morning. Her father, R. C. Morrow, a share-cropper who made the trip each week to purchase supplies, had relented and let her three young brothers go to town with him, but only if she would come along to keep an eye on them while he conducted business. Thinking she'd get away from the never-ending list of chores awaiting her on the farm, Ilene had agreed.

Dalton was instantly smitten with his sister's friend. He couldn't help noticing that Ilene appeared a little breathless herself. They talked until Ilene spotted her father heading toward them. Since Ilene was only sixteen and not yet allowed to date or even to talk to boys without an adult present, she jumped back onto the wagon and whispered goodbye.

The following Monday, Dalton wrote a short letter to the girl who had haunted his thoughts and invaded his dreams for two days and nights. His sister addressed the envelope for him and he mailed it that same afternoon.

Fate intervened on Thursday evening when Ilene was asked to walk down the long dirt driveway to collect the mail. She was surprised to see something addressed to her and decided on impulse to read it before returning to the house. She stared flabbergasted at the simple words written by the soft-spoken soldier who had filled her thoughts all week.

Ilene Morrow,

If you want to get married, I'll be waiting at the same spot in town next Saturday.

Signed,
Dalton F. Williams

Saturday morning rolled around with a brilliant sky full of sunshine and dreams of the future. During the last two days, the secret note had been reread a thousand times and finally, just before daybreak, on the fateful day, a decision was reached. As her father readied everything for the customary trip into town, Ilene eagerly changed into her best dress and volunteered to go along and look after her younger siblings.

At the exact moment the unsuspecting farmer walked into the general store, a 1939 Ford pulled up beside the wagon and honked the horn. Dalton sat behind the oversized wheel wearing a big smile. His brother and sister-in-law were squeezed into the backseat to act as witnesses. With a sense of adventure, and a heart pierced by Cupid, Ilene grabbed her purse and jumped off the weathered wagon seat. She kissed her puzzled brothers goodbye and slid into the front seat of the shiny black car that would whisk her away from childhood and transform her into a woman.

When the cheerful group arrived in the nearby town of Rising Fawn, Georgia, they discovered the law required a female to be eighteen years old before a wedding ceremony could be performed without her parents' consent. Naturally, Ilene became distraught. She grew more anxious as the time approached for the nuptials to be spoken, because as much as she longed to marry Dalton, she had grown up in a Christian home where lying was strictly forbidden.

When the clerk called for the next couple to come forward, Ilene mumbled a hasty excuse and stepped into the next room. She scribbled the number "18" on a small slip of paper, placed it in the bottom of her right shoe—making sure it was firmly underneath her foot—and then returned to the room where everyone waited.

The overworked justice of the peace barely looked up as he skeptically asked, "Are you eighteen yet, miss?"

Ilene replied with a twinkle in her eyes, "I am over eighteen."

She repeated her vows with a clear conscience, knowing she had told the truth. When she later confessed to her new husband, Dalton was delighted his bride had such high morals as well as being so resourceful.

Before my father passed on, my parents had four children and spent fifty-four years together in the same small town where they met and fell in love. Dad taught us to love and appreciate our roots, and Mom instilled a sense of decency in us, sprinkled with a light dose of creativity.

I met my husband, Tim, in this same friendly town where we have both lived all of our lives and will forever call home. We have spent the past eighteen years raising our three children and following my parents' wonderful example. ೲ

Church on the Hill

by Arthur Bowler | *Randolph, Massachusetts*

THEY SAY YOU CAN'T GO HOME AGAIN, but at the age of thirty-eight, after many years far from home, I attempted to do exactly that. I had led an eventful life with more than a dozen odd jobs from Santa Claus to radio DJ to English teacher. I had driven alone across the North American continent twice in an old Volkswagen beetle, and had traveled solo through Europe before ending up in the United Kingdom, where I met my wife—a shy Swiss girl who had gone there to learn English and ended up with a husband. Now, after several years in Switzerland, I felt the need to do something more meaningful and to go home again. Of all the jobs I'd had, I missed only two of them: son and brother.

Randolph, Massachusetts, is not a particularly special place, yet it was here that I marched in the school band on Memorial Day, swooshed down Main Street in countless snowstorms, and sneaked a first look at *Playboy* behind the school. My heart, although once broken by Mary Edwards, was still there, as was the "church on the hill," as it was widely known. Over the years, the old meetinghouse had been an integral part of my life and the lives of the townspeople.

◄◦►

In earlier times, town meetings were held there, and one afternoon in 1812, 400 men gathered on the front lawn to face off with British squadrons near the coast. Today, the white church on the highest point in town remains an important landmark; a source of orientation, in one way or another, especially for me. It was here that I hoped to return to work as a minister-in-training and as a student at Harvard Divinity School, alongside my parents. My father had been the minister since 1956, and my mother had been the organist and choir director for just as long.

So my Swiss-American family packed up a few things, including one baby daughter, and started a new life in the new world. I couldn't wait to enter the old meetinghouse again. When I did, a flood of memories returned. I smelled lilies on Easter morning, saw red and green decorations on Christmas Eve, and felt the warm embrace of almost-forgotten friends. I remembered square dances, harvest fairs, and bean suppers; but even more, I remembered the sense of community that was there. Together we had faced the triumphs and the tragedies. We had lived, and loved, together. Of course, some things about the town and church were different. Yet, as I stood shoulder to shoulder with my dad on Sunday mornings, I was home and felt boundless pride in my family, my hometown, and my country.

Three years later, in an unusual experience, my father ordained me into the ministry in the church of my youth as my mother played the organ, both of them long past normal retirement age. A local newspaper chronicled the event with a photograph of my father and me standing in front of the house of worship with a pineapple above the door, an old colonial symbol of welcome.

They—my town, my church, my family—had welcomed their wayfaring son home. But it was not to be forever. Before long, fate carried me back to the other side of the ocean again.

These days, when I find myself swallowing a bit harder on Christmas Eve, I remind myself that life means change, and it can be nostalgic. Instead of being sad, I try to treasure the time I went home again, and I know that every one of us can do it too—if not literally, at least in the heart. ∾

Another Summer's End

by Sharon Cupp Pennington | *Trinity, Texas*

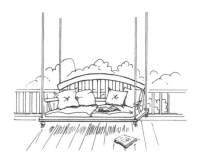

ON THE WIDE-PLANKED PORCH of my grandfather's house, I savor an invigorating breath of country air. No smog, no stench from paper mills or refineries belching grimy steam to irritate the sinuses or coat the throat with cloying fumes.

I fold the jacket of my suit over one arm, look down at my feet, and smile as I wiggle my toes inside the sheer nylons. I've come home, and memories flood my mind.

I'm suddenly seven years old again and stand barefoot next to the tank of lukewarm water alive with darting minnows. "Lift me up, Grandpa. Let me see." The day is clear, the sun high and hot, but not nearly as hot as a month ago. Seasons change so fast. Almost Labor Day, 1955, and the end has come, too soon, to the best summer of my life.

From the highway below, another fisherman bound for the Trinity River pulls into Grandpa's sprawling yard to buy bait and with it, an ice-cold melon or two. In dusty cars and boat-towing trucks they have come in a steady stream since sunrise.

"City folk," he calls them. But not with anger or disrespect. Grandpa seldom raises his voice.

The men wear funny hats with shiny lures attached like Christmas ornaments, and khaki vests with more pockets than I can count or they could possibly fill. Some smoke cigarettes. Others puff on pipes smelling of wood smoke and vanilla. They chat with Grandpa, busy at the tank. He dips the little net and scoops the slippery, silvery fish, then drops them in water he's poured into dull metal buckets.

He gives me a huge grin and winks, like there's a magical secret between us. But, then, everything about Grandpa Fred is magical, from his shirt pocket stuffed with candied orange slices to the blue baseball cap shoved high on his head of salt-and-pepper hair, and that includes the silly jokes that make Grandma Minnie's cheeks turn pink.

He moves to the covered tank on the other side of the oak tree, its shade already shrinking, and lifts the lid. This tank smells different. Not tinny like the minnow tank, like its high walls are lined with old nickels, but earthy and dank. He reaches in with a callused hand and turns the rich, moist soil. A dozen earthworms struggle to rebury themselves.

I squeal and laugh, caught up in the excitement a child finds in a sticky Texas afternoon and a handful of wriggling worms. Grandpa laughs, too.

"Our Sherry's got potential," he tells the tall man with the dark glasses and snowy beard. "Smart as a whip; she's gonna be somebody."

I think how lucky I am to have this day, this great summer, to be Grandpa's girl—to have potential, although I'm not sure what potential is. All I know is it feels good when Grandpa says it.

Grandpa's girl . . .

I pull the door to the house shut, not bothering to lock it. This isn't the city. I turn slowly and take another look around the yard, beyond the now empty and corroded bait tanks to the few sparse acres of Grandpa's farm. There's much to be done if we're to bring it back.

My husband smiles from the front seat of the dusty Chevrolet parked on the gravel-topped driveway. In the backseat, our daughter clutches her worn Cabbage Patch doll and presses her nose against the glass. She looks a lot like I did on that August day so many summers ago.

Reluctantly, I slip on my shoes and take the first of three concrete steps down. Butterflies flit in and out of newly cleared beds of roses and nodding day lilies. The gnarled walnut tree stands near the gate, surrogate patriarch to all Grandpa cherished. His legacy to me, and now to my child. Trailing vines of purple four-o'clocks, their blooms partially closed, climb the stone-lined path to the sloping porch. I embrace the familiar ache in my heart. When I take hold of the wooden rail, I know it will still be loose. I think we'll leave it that way—some things should never change. ∼

The Town of Trinity, Texas

Population: 2,700

Saving Beloved Old Red

Trinity's abandoned schoolhouse, called Old Red because of the red bricks, recently received a face-lift when former students and towns-folk rallied together and formed the Save Old Red Committee, raising $100,000 to restore the building's exterior. The remodeling crews, many of which included former students, copied and replaced the ninety-one wooden windows in the building. The Trinity Independent School District is currently working on the interior remodeling.

Old Red served as Trinity's only school building until 1928. At that time, a second two-story structure was built to house the town's junior high and high school. The new building was built in the shape of a *T* to capture wind from any direction it might blow into town. ❧

Town Facts

First incorporated: Trinity was founded in the winter of 1872–1873 on land purchased from the New York and Texas Land Company.

Transportation: Rail and automobile

Location: Eighty-one miles north of Houston. The Trinity River runs two miles southwest of the town, and at one time, the land the town of Trinity occupies was part of the Trinity River basin and completely submerged in water.

Former names: The first documented settlement in the vicinity was called Kayser's Prairie. Later, it was renamed Trinity Station, after the Trinity River. The name was later changed to Trinity City, and finally to Trinity.

May 20, 1873—Trinity became the county seat. Though the title moved to the town of Pennington in 1874, Trinity remained a railroad center and the largest town in the county.

1906—Alex McDonald had built the first light plant in Trinity in 1906. He had two Fairbank-Morse generators. This plant was destroyed when downtown Trinity burned in 1909. McDonald also operated the first picture show in Trinity. It was because of his need for electricity in the theatre that the town is indebted to the MacDonald family for the first electricity in Trinity.

1909—Business section destroyed by fire, but the town rebuilt and incorporated in 1910. Trinity suffered another fire in 1915, and incorporated again the following year.

1914—Population had climbed to 1,800.

Of Outlaws and Hospitality

The infamous outlaw John Wesley Hardin, the son of a Methodist preacher, was once shot during a game in a Trinity saloon. Following the shooting incident, he and his friends slipped out of town and stopped at the home of George and Elzirah (White) Gibson, where Hardin's friends asked for help for what they said was a "sick man" in the wagon. Naturally, being good folks, the Gibsons immediately offered a pillow and pillowcase to make the sick man more comfortable. It wasn't until the wagon was long gone that the couple learned the sick man was actually John Wesley Hardin. Not too long thereafter, the Gibsons reported that their pillow and pillowcase were returned, freshly laundered.

Years later, Trinity had another visitor who was on the wrong side of the law. This time it was Clyde Barrow, the male half of the Bonnie-and-Clyde duo. Clyde came through Trinity on his way to nearby Eastham Prison Farm to break out gang member Raymond Hamilton. ✍

The Old Lady's Field

by Marie D. Jones | *Garnerville, New York*

THE TINY TOWN OF Garnerville, New York, is nothing but a speck on a speck on a speck on a map; a woodsy hamlet about forty-five minutes north of New York City, nestled in the delicious greenery of Rockland County. But to me, Garnerville was a hotbed of legends, myths, and tall tales, a truly magical place for a kid with a huge imagination to grow up in.

When I was a child in the early '60s, growing up in Garnerville meant coffee klatches, block parties, kids walking alone without fear, and seven P.M. air raid sirens announcing the coming of night. It was small-town America at its finest, close enough to the big city to feel the hip influence, yet far enough away to keep the innocence and natural purity intact.

Our little house sat upon a wonderfully named street: Captain Shankey Drive. Behind us was a huge expanse of woods and a lake we called our own. One of our favorite pastimes as kids was walking to the local candy and ice cream shop, a quaint two-story house on Main Street called Red's. Red really did have red hair, and penny candies galore. If you got to go to Red's with a quarter, you could literally bring back enough loot to last you, well, the *whole* morning!

There were only two routes to get to Red's. One was to walk all the way down the long and winding Captain Shankey Drive to Main Street, which was not a problem except for the fact that you had to walk back up Captain Shankey on the way home. The other route was the shortcut through a place that sent chills up and down the spines of children all over the neighborhood, a place that had become legend: The Old Lady's Field.

It was a large expanse of empty land, with brown grass that sometimes grew taller than we kids were. At the opposite end of the field was a rambling, white, two-story house with a porch and some rundown cars parked askew. This was the Old Lady's house, and that stretch of land that meant cutting our trip to Red's in half was her field. Rumor had it she was a witch—an evil witch.

For those of us brave enough to challenge the legend, it meant going quietly and tightly in small groups across the far perimeter of the Old Lady's Field. We held on to each other's hands for dear life, dreading each and every second. We wondered when the beast herself would emerge from her domain bearing a shotgun and accompanied by a vicious German shepard, which we often heard barking from a distance.

We rarely cut through the Old Lady's Field. But on occasion, when it was just too hot to walk the longer route, we risked our lives to sneak through the field, darting past the metal NO TRESPASSING signs, not able to breathe again until the sights and sounds of Main Street appeared.

Rumor had it that the Old Lady shot some older kids cutting through her domain. And legend had it her dog bit off a teenager's foot when the Old Lady caught the poor, unfortunate soul on her land. And on Halloween, when the field beckoned like a silent graveyard, myths abounded about stupid kids who dared venture into the dark field, never to be seen or heard from again.

Funny thing is, not once did we ever encounter the Old Lady. Even when my dad took us for a drive up Route 202, which passed right in front of the Old Lady's house, we never saw her coming out with gun in hand, pointing a crooked finger at us and shouting vicious accusations. In fact, we never saw her at all. And when we questioned the adults in the neighborhood, they were sure they had never seen her, either.

As for the German shepherd, I did see a little wiener dog in the yard once, on one of Dad's drive-bys, barking and yapping incessantly. But never did the wicked, evil witch who tortured and tormented hundreds of innocent children emerge.

In the '70s, my family moved to the West Coast. After a twenty-year absence, I went back to my old neighborhood hidden amidst the woodlands along the mighty Hudson River. Everything was the same on Captain Shankey Drive. Most of the people who had lived there when I was a resident, still remained. The houses looked the same. The woods and lake were still there. The quaint, small-town feeling of knowing the names of all your neighbors was still present.

But two things were long gone. Red's had been sold years before, and was now just somebody's house on Main Street. And the Old Lady's Field had been plowed and paved and parceled, and now housed about two dozen spanking new homes.

I still laugh in wonder about that strange, yet persistent hometown legend and stories that refused to die despite any lack of evidence or first-person witnesses. No longer would the kids of Captain Shankey Drive have the terrifying challenge, or the weird pleasure, of tempting fate and the Old Lady as they cut through her field on the way to get some cheap candy.

The place I live in now has no legends. It is a new development with no history. I only know a handful of my neighbors. Kids never play outside without an adult. There is no nearby field, or woods, or lake to be explored, just a lot of houses that all look the same. And there is no such thing as penny candy anymore.

It all makes me sad. If I think about it too hard, it makes me grumpy, and I can't help but wonder if the neighborhood children, who occasionally sneak through my yard, will one day refer to me as the evil Old Lady.

Christmas Pet

by Carol McAdoo Rehme | *Arkansas City, Kansas*

"HOME FOR THE HOLIDAYS" meant more to me that year than merely nostalgic words in a seasonal carol. It meant family, friends, and reminiscences of Christmases past. It meant an opportunity to tour my old neighborhood in Arkansas City, Kansas, home of my youth.

As we passed the schoolyard, I noticed the stately cottonwood still stood sentinel on the dusty playground. It was shorter than I remembered and not as broad. Adams Elementary seemed to have shrunk, too. But the memories loomed as large as ever, one in particular. I stifled a smile as my fourth-grade classroom came into view in my mind's eye.

The radiator hissed contentedly as I plowed my pencil into a wood furrow in the scarred desk top, deepening an *X* carved by a previous tenant. Behind me, assorted midwinter sniffles and coughs punctuated Quiet Time.

Thumbing the pages of my reader, I stole a look around the classroom. My gaze lingered on the brown paper bags squatting beneath the chairs of my two best friends. I didn't have to peek at the wire rack under my own to know a third sack waited there. I was uncomfortably aware; I couldn't ignore it if I wanted to. And, believe me, I wanted to.

The first day back to school was made more difficult by the January drab that trailed last month's glitter. Carrot-nosed snowmen no longer danced down the corridor walls. No red and green balls bobbed from the ceiling, no stained-glass artwork gleamed in the windows, no jeweled trees winked from the bulletin boards. Even the spicy scent of clove-studded oranges had evaporated along with the decorations. There were no remnants to show that the holidays had come and gone.

Yet the evidence lurked in those bags and I dreaded the moment of reckoning. My heart beat in the same halting rhythm as the second hand on the big wall clock. Only seven minutes left until recess and the unveiling.

During the weeks prior to Christmas, Pam, Gayle, and I had shared the same wish. Instead of sugarplums, our heads danced with dreams of *The Kitty.* You know the one, the kitty with white powder-puff fur to rub against your cheek, and unblinking topaz eyes that promised to keep secrets—the same kitty whose palm-sized body was perfect for nestling in a young girl's hand. You know, the stuffed kitty everyone craved that December in the '50s.

The three of us plotted our strategy well. In the earliest days, we did extra chores. We were cheerful and obliging. We dropped careful hints. We circled the kitten's description in J.C. Penney's Winter Catalog, to ensure against imitations. As Christmas drew nearer, we forged into Phase Two of our plan—reminding, bargaining, pleading—whining to our parents that everyone else would be getting one. Nothing was beneath us.

At my house, Mother was too busy with the new baby to Christmas shop. Instead, she handed Daddy her detailed list, pecked his cheek, and shooed him out the door. This could be good, I thought. As a shopper, Daddy was inexperienced but methodical.

He would follow the list, no questions asked, and I already knew what was on it because I had peeked—Phase Three. My kitty was a sure thing.

Following tradition, we opened presents one at a time on Christmas Eve. Since I had rattled, squeezed, and prodded each and every gift tagged with my name, I knew for certain which package held the kitten. I saved it for last.

The entire family watched. I knew they felt my excitement. Shiny gold foil crinkled when my hands pressed the shape of it. Long pieces of Scotch tape curled under as my nails bit into the packaging. A bit of soft white fur feathered the folded edge. Eyes closed, I slid my fingers inside to let them brush across a butter-soft nose, trace the length of tiny felt ears, and curl into luxurious fur. Smiling, I tugged away the wrappings and opened my eyes to . . . a stuffed skunk?

It was a skunk, all right, complete with long white stripe, beady black eyes, and squatty little ears. I looked up—directly into Daddy's anxious grin—only half hearing his garbled explanation of lengthy store lines, empty shelves, and the exhaustive hunt for a suitable substitution. It felt like a giant snowball had settled in my stomach. I was a heartsick nine-year-old, torn between the crush of my own disappointment and a deep-rooted desire to keep the eager smile on my daddy's face.

"When I saw this, I couldn't believe my eyes," he gushed.

Me neither, I thought.

"Just wait until the other kids see this," he said.

Can't wait, I thought.

"Why, I'll bet you're the only girl in the whole school who got a skunk this Christmas!" Daddy nodded happily. "You'll be different."

No kidding, I thought. This really stinks.

Even so, I swallowed back the tears, walked across the room to hug Daddy, and whispered a broken thank-you in his ear.

Now, as the harsh bell signaled recess, would come the unveiling.

Pam, Gayle, and I made our pilgrimage to the thick trunk of the ancient cottonwood where we were shielded from the knife-edged wind. Like the Magi bearing gifts, we knelt beneath the tree. Pam opened her paper bag first. Reverently, she offered her palm-sized kitten with the topaz eyes. "I call her Snowball."

Gayle was second. She cupped an identical ball of pristine white fluff. "I named mine Marshmallow."

By this time, all the other fourth-grade girls circled us, admiring and cooing. It was my turn. "Well, I named mine—Stinky!" I blurted. With a hard swallow, I jerked back the rolled flap of the wrinkled brown sack, grabbed the sack by the bottom, and shook out the awful black skunk. In the silence that seemed to last forever, I glanced up. Wide-eyed girls stared at Stinky. There were a few scattered giggles and then they all started to chatter at once.

"A skunk! He's so cute!"

"Can I see him?"

"Why, he's made out of genuine rabbit fur!"

"Pass him over here. Oh look, you can make his tail bend."

"I wish I'd gotten one of those."

Flushing as bright as Rudolf's nose, I combed my fingers through the skunk's fur. Girls pressed nearer, huddled against the cold, to ask questions and beg for chances to hold the unparalleled pet.

Suddenly Pam turned to Gayle. "Why, I bet she's the only girl in the whole school who got a skunk for Christmas!"

Thanks to Daddy, my grin stretched from ear to ear. ∼

Persimmon Memories

by Sylvia Nickels | *Temple, Georgia*

"MAMOM. LOOK AT THESE OLD PICTURES," my granddaughter, Briana, said as she moved along the wall of the truck stop examining the dozen or so large-framed black-and-white prints that chronicled the history of Temple, Georgia. Pointing to one picture she asked, "What's that?"

I moved beside her and smiled. "It's the old cotton gin. It was across the railroad track." As though summoned by my words, the loud wail of a diesel engine sounded outside, followed by the *whump, whump, whump* of dozens of boxcars passing over uneven cross ties.

Bri covered her ears. "Good Lord. How do they stand it?"

I smiled as the memories began to unfold. "When I was a child, steam engines pulled long lines of railcars—the last a red caboose—along the track over there. I'd stand in the cotton fields and listen to their whistles, and a little later the drawn-out lament of powerful diesels."

She must have caught the nostalgia in my words, because she grinned mischievously. "What else are you remembering?"

"I dreamed of boarding one of the sleek passenger trains to the big city and exciting adventures. I so wanted to ride the one I'd heard called the *Nancy Hanks* to Savannah and see the Atlantic Ocean. Or maybe those rails could take me across Alabama, and the other states between me and the Mississippi, all the way to the Pacific, like de Soto."

A puzzled look crossed her face then, as if she was trying to picture my childhood but couldn't. "What was it like? Did the whole family have to pick cotton?"

"If we were about six or older. We had to try and get it picked before it got rained on. Those rows of cotton, shoulder-high to me, looked endless. By the time it was ready for picking, the pods had got hard and needle-tipped. They pricked our fingers and left red spots on the cotton sometimes.

"Every evening we dumped the baskets of cotton on one end of the porch. Boards were nailed between the posts for a few feet up to keep the cotton from blowing away. We knew we weren't supposed to, but we liked to jump and roll on it. Packed down cotton didn't sell for as much money. If we were caught, we got a switching on bare legs. When the pile of cotton was a bale, about three hundred pounds, I think, Daddy and Papaw hauled it to the gin."

"Look, there's a pile of cotton on a horse-drawn wagon," Bri said pointing to another picture. "Was that how it was brought to the gin?"

"Sure was. But look again, those are mules. They were better for farm work, stronger."

The scattered group of houses that filled the next frame took me back to my grandmother's porch. Several of the houses had long, L-shaped wraparound porches like the one we piled cotton on at Mamaw's. Hers always blazed, spring and summer, with pots of crimson geraniums, orange marigolds, and petunias in every hue of the rainbow.

Bri pointed to a print that showed a woman scattering something from a bucket, a flock of chickens around her feet. "Did they have barns and livestock, even in town?"

I nodded. "There were no supermarkets then and only a few stores besides the gin. Even in town, people raised most of their food."

After we'd eaten, Bri strayed back toward the old pictures. "It's not far to the place where you lived when you were little, is it, Mamom?"

I glanced up at her, my eyes hopeful. "If we go by there, we won't get to LaGrange before dark."

"That's okay. I'd like to see where you grew up."

I took the now paved state road to the winding country lane leading to the farm that had once belonged to my mother's uncle, which we had farmed on shares for him. I could not even find the site of the little house where we'd lived or where the barn had stood, but I described them for Bri in great detail for they remain vivid in my memory. I explained how we scattered corn for the chickens, and collected eggs from the nests in the shed. In the fall, we didn't worry about disturbing the setting hens. The chicks that had hatched in the spring were pullets and half-grown roosters. The ones who survived Sunday and holiday dinners, through the winter, produced their own eggs and chicks the next spring.

The fattened hogs, in ignorance of their fate, grunted and rooted for acorns in the hog pen a little way from the house. They were slaughtered early on the morning of the first hard frost. Hams and shoulders were hoisted from the rafters in the smokehouse, and sausage and pickled feet were canned to provide meat for winter.

I showed her the 'simmon (persimmon) tree across the road from the hog pen. With the first frost the green fruit changed from mouth-drawing bitterness to gooey orange-red pulp.

"We'd stand under the tree, stuffing them in our orange-stained mouths. They were rich and sweet as sugar." I shook my head with the memory and sighed. "Yum." Bri listened intently as I relived my childhood. "Oh, the pecan trees are still here, those two tall ones over there, Bri. We raced the squirrels for the pecans, but they got their share at night."

Other childhood memories gently surfaced in my mind as I walked with my granddaughter along the dusty unpaved lane.

"The smell of bacon and Mamaw's biscuits baking in the wood-fired stove pulled us awake. We begged for 'soaky' biscuits—biscuits soaked in weak coffee and sprinkled with sugar."

Briana took my hand as we walked to the car. "Your memories, like the 'simmons, grow sweeter with the frost of years, don't they, Mamom?"

Misty-eyed, I squeezed her hand. "A precious granddaughter who is charmed by her Mamom's ancient history sure adds to that sweetness." 🙰

Forty Birkhead Place

by Lynn Ruth Miller | *Toledo, Ohio*

WHEN I WAS NINE YEARS OLD, my father discovered an old two-story stucco house in a small, gated community of stately homes once owned by the very rich. We had always lived in small apartments and this house seemed like a castle to us. So many rooms! So many places to play!

The house was my mother's dream made real. It had a master bedroom as large as our whole apartment on Islington Street, with a dressing room for her and another for my father. There were four smaller bedrooms upstairs and a playroom for my sister and me to keep ourselves amused in. I had a whole wall of bookshelves to fill with books. What more could a little girl want?

The kitchen had a table big enough for us all to eat breakfast and watch my mother assemble the ingredients for the meals to come. My mother's art was her cooking, and when I think of Forty Birkhead Place, I remember aromatic briskets, chopped eggplant in olive oil, and chicken soup with *matzo* balls so light I expected them to fly from the pot into our soup bowls without benefit of a ladle. And then there were the desserts: floating island yellow and creamy with clouds of meringue on top, chocolate cake so magnificent that the very aroma brought all the neighbor children to our door. Yes, memories of that house are memories of foods no restaurant could equal.

But the best part of our house was the basement with the paneled recreation room, laundry room, and fruit cellar filled with dilled pickles, tomatoes, apple butter, and canned vegetables from our garden. You didn't have to go down the basement to get into that storage area. Instead you could go out the kitchen door and open the most wonderful aperture ever invented by man: the cellar door.

How many times did my cousin and I slide down that magic cellar door? How many times did we grit our teeth and suffer silently while our mothers pried slivers from our bottoms? And how many times did we invent elaborate shows for the neighbors in that lavish backyard with its trees of buckeye, cherry, and apple? We made costumes out of mother's castoffs, and crepe paper bonnets to cover our pigtails. We waved flags and made bright banners to herald all the neighbors to an off-key musical filled with nonsense only children could create.

I have lived in well over a dozen houses since I left Forty Birkhead Place, but I have never had another home. Home was huge family dinner parties in that noble dining room under the crystal chandelier. Home was a climbing rose on the side of the garage and a purple maple tree that grew taller each year. Home was the Chickering piano in the living room where I spent hours practicing from the day I was nine years old until I graduated from Scott High School and left for Ann Arbor to conquer the world. I sat before that bay window on a yellow print couch every weekend waiting for my date to pick me up and open the door to romance.

I can still feel the excitement that was always there for me in that white stucco house with the maroon-trimmed windows. I can still hear the swing music on the old Victrola. I can still see the little brick road that led to our driveway and hear our neighbor, Mary Kaplan, singing her scales in the house next door. It is all there and I relive it every time I close my eyes.

Last year, I went back to see the place that had defined my childhood. I drove through the rusted gates into the cluster of houses that had once been filled with people I knew, and rounded the bend to number forty. Suddenly, as if by magic, I was a child once more. I looked at the home, barely altered by the years. A tricycle—very like the one I had, with red ribbons on the handlebars—sat in the drive. The maple was far larger now and almost concealed that blessed screened-in porch where we all sat together on the glider, swinging our legs and enjoying what breeze there was to be found on scorching August nights.

Forty Birkhead Place. I stood outside its front door and the past enveloped me like a comforting feather blanket. Swing music wafted from the living room, and could it be? Yes! I would know the sound anywhere. Mary Kaplan was singing her scales, the notes like tinkling bells to remind me of all I had left behind. ᑐ

See the USA

by Kimberly A. Porrazzo | *Fountain Valley, California*

DURING THE SUMMER OF '67, at the age of ten, I saw America from the right rear window of my dad's ocean-blue Chevy BelAir station wagon. Thirty-seven years later, I can still feel the hot desert air brush my cheek as I flip the pages of our family photo album. I can still hear the fish slapping the water while flopping on the end of my line as we dropped our poles into the lakes of upstate New York. And the taste of Islay's ice cream, slurped up while giggling with my East Coast cousins on that humid Pennsylvania night, is fresh on my tongue. The memories are as fresh as the morning Dad turned on the ignition and said, "Let's go."

Silly recollections come to mind, like my thighs sticking to the vinyl backseat after hours on the road, to the thrill of sighting the Statue of Liberty with eyes as fresh as my Italian immigrant grandfather's. . . . These are the moments that make a trip across America a family adventure and one of the sweetest memories one can own.

On our six-week trek from the small town of Fountain Valley, a quiet bedroom community in Southern California, we traveled northeast through dusty St. George, Utah, where we spent our first night in the fourteen-foot Travel Queen trailer that would be our summer home. A day or so later, the lush Black Hills of South Dakota and the first glimpse of Mt. Rushmore were just the beginning of a tour of all that is great in this country, big and small. Historical sites swarmed with tourists and endless landscapes dotted here and there with country farms came and went as we continued our journey. I soaked up the contrast between quaint towns resembling Andy Griffith's lily-white Mayberry and the concrete stoops of the Bronx where as we passed through, trailer in tow, we were under surveillance by suspicious eyes.

Tracing the route that AAA planned for us during the same summer that TV commercials for Chevrolet were singing, "See the USA in your Chevrolet," I moved along a collection of images eternally seared into my head. There was that fancy French restaurant in Montreal where, for the first time, a waiter put a napkin on my lap for me. In the scorching month of August, we sizzled on the asphalt campground just outside of Manhattan in between tours of the city. My legs grew weary as I recalled counting the steps inside the Washington Monument. Was it 867? In Gettysburg, I stood on the same platform that Abe Lincoln stood on more than a hundred years earlier, when he began, "Four score and seven years ago. . . ." Farther south, I kept careful watch for the blue grass in Kentucky, but after hours of driving it all looked green to me. And my older brother and I counted endless license plates in between backseat fights, as Route 66 led us back to Southern California.

I saw firsthand what makes a family on that trip. My dad, a school principal, was at the helm. I was safe wherever we went as long as Dad was with us. Mom held the maps and directed our course. She also handled the money, her large black purse never leaving the crook of her arm. My brother and I entertained each other as kids do, making up word games and singing silly songs. We laughed. We fought. We slept. We watched as America passed our car windows like a National Geographic slide show.

During that summer, our family's Chevy BelAir wagon was our portal to America. Eight thousand miles later, we were home.

Back in Fountain Valley, the friendly little city whose slogan is ". . . a nice place to live," our lives resumed. Piano lessons, Sunday mass, and high school football games punctuated each week. Soon after, I attended our local state college where I met my sweetheart, whom I later married. We now have two sons.

I count that family vacation among my most cherished memories. Not only did I see so much of what makes up our great country, but I learned how important my own hometown is to me. There's no place I'd rather be.

Home Is Where Mama Is

by Gay Wiggin-Comboy | *Gravette, Arkansas*

MY FIRST JOURNEY AWAY from my childhood home in Gravette, Arkansas, was at the age of eleven. It had been a long, hot summer, which I had spent helping my oldest sister with her new baby. I didn't know how homesick I was until they dropped me off in front of the house.

I stood with suitcase in hand at the gate of the white picket fence. Excitement mounted inside me. I wanted to run up the sidewalk, jump up the step onto the front porch, open the door, and holler, "Mama!" Instead, I walked slowly, so I wouldn't miss any of the sights. The green birdbath still sat beside my climbing tree, a wasp buzzed around the large tree with our tire swing, the metal chairs and swing were on the porch for evening sitting.

The heat of the afternoon was suffocating. Perspiration made my dress feel sticky-damp, but as I stepped into the living room the air turned cool and crisp, making my wet dress feel cooler. I lingered to let my eyes adjust to the dim interior. The house was quiet except for the hum of Mama's large fan sitting in the west window where the old trees shaded and cooled that side of the house. The green tile floor shone from layers of wax, the green walls almost matched. Even thought my mother wasn't home, the house was surrounded by the feel of her.

The moment was broken when my older sister Betty burst through the kitchen door to greet me, but the feelings lingered on.

I grew up and moved to Lee's Summit, Missouri, and every time I returned home, as I drove those curvy Arkansas roads, the excitement mounted up in me as if I were eleven years old again.

My one request of Mama: "Don't ever sell the house, so I can always come home."

Years later, when my stepfather died, my mother remarried and felt she had to ask my permission to sell the house. My sisters, their husbands, a nephew, and I worked on the house to get it ready for the real estate market. After everyone left at the end of the day, I lingered a little longer.

When Mama came to get me, we walked through the house for the last time. I told her I wished I would have a couple of days more to work on it so it would be in perfect shape, and she smiled knowingly.

Now, when I go see Mama, I always swing by to see the home place in Gravette. It's getting older and seems smaller, but I still remember the feeling of the beautiful home of my childhood days. Then I whiz on down the road to Mama's new home, and I realize the warmth of home is wherever my mother lives. ᐦ

Granny's Garden Hat

by Elaine Ernst Schneider | *Mesquite, Texas*

GRANNY'S DEATH WAS HARD FOR ME. The funeral was especially hard. I had smiled weakly and thanked everyone for coming, but my hurt was deeper than that which showed on the surface. It was more than the tears, more than the lines of grief that pinched my face and drew my stomach into knots. It was the thought that I would have to walk into the front yard that led to Granny's tiny house, knowing she wouldn't be there.

Since I had been a little girl, going to Granny's house meant a delightful trek to the country. Mesquite was a small town forty years ago—just a little dot on the Texas map—and Granny's home was on the outskirts of town. The white frame house was small but adequate. There were wooden floors, and glass knobs on all the doors and cabinets. The gas stove in the kitchen was older than my mother, but Granny had cooked up "good eating" like she didn't know any better. Turnip greens and cabbage were specialties of the house.

As a child, I had loved to walk through the wildflowers out back, but was allowed to do so only in the company of my grandmother, who always carried a hoe. Sometimes we saw jackrabbits and ground hogs. Other times, a snake slithered by on a hunt for a rat. That's what the hoe was for. On a few occasions, Granny chopped off the head of an unfriendly copperhead. She taught me to freeze when she whistled. That meant wildlife was near. "We want to blend into the scenery," she had said. But many times the air was simply too full to remain quiet. The bees hummed, the frogs rumbled, and Granny and I would cut loose, chirping along with the birds in a contest to see who could sing louder.

Though I loved everything about Granny's place, my favorite was her front-yard flowerbed. It was there that we planted an "on-purpose" patch of flowers. This bed always brimmed with irises in bright hues of yellow and purple, waving in the country breeze. No wonder Granny named them her flags. It was this flowerbed that I dreaded seeing. I knew the memories would be pungent.

The trip to Granny's house seemed longer than I remembered. I scanned the roadside as I drove, wanting to see things as Granny had last seen them. When I arrived, I sighed with relief. Not so much had changed. Despite Mesquite's growth as a city, the area where my grandmother had lived still boasted small but comfortable homes with shaded driveways, porches filled with potted plants, and dogs that yapped in the yards.

I pulled into Granny's driveway and parked. I saw it right off, of course, the flowerbed of irises waving at me, beckoning me to come and relive old times. But I couldn't face them. Instead, I walked into the garage, fervently peeking around every corner for the rat or snake that might lie in hiding now that the hoe hung owner-less on the pegboard above my head. Seeing that hoe brought on an emptiness and loss that was all-consuming. I turned to leave, tearing at spider webs and wondering why they thought they had a right to be there. Thrashing like a crazed and frightened child, I wasn't paying much attention to what I batted down from the walls. Bugs, bird nests, garden tools—all of it came tumbling down.

Straw grazed my cheek as Granny's garden hat dropped from a shelf that my tirade had jarred loose. Bending down, I grasped it, held it to my chest for a moment, and then plopped the thing—dirt, spider webs, and all—right onto my head, pulling the brim down over my eyes like Granny used to do. Equipped with Granny's gardening hat, I turned toward the flowerbed.

Stomping into the irises, I kicked at the pot that I had once used to plant the seeds my grandmother gleaned for me. It shattered at my feet and I sat down on the hard ground and sobbed shamefully. It was only then that I saw it—an earthworm. The worm hadn't noticed me and was slowly winding its way through the disheveled garden mess I had created. It was headed underground, but what must have seemed a massive obstacle loomed in its way— the proverbial bump in the road. A piece of the broken pot stood in the way of the worm's progress. The earthworm paused and assessed its situation. Then it concentrated on the bump until it was able to get past it.

I ran my fingers across the rough edge of Granny's hat and I suddenly understood what the earthworm had always known. Life would go on without my grandmother's home-cooked meals. Someone else would walk over the wooden floors of her house. A new face would peer across her fence, and the chatter of good neighbors would no longer include her input. Fresh friendships would form. And the city of Mesquite would no doubt grow, perhaps engulfing even her small-town neighborhood. But the memories of country air and irises waving hello—or goodbye—could remain with me forever. And just like my newfound friend, Mr. Earthworm, I would move on with my life, one memory, and one bump, at a time. ✑

Home Sweet Home

by CJ Nyman | *Felton, California*

As I slowly headed up the steep hill, I glanced from side to side and smiled. Felton, California, didn't seem to have changed. Though it had been years since I left the summer cabin, it was as if the world had stood still in my absence. The names on the mailboxes were the same, the cabins a little more sheltered by larger shrubs, perhaps, but recognizable. So, naturally, I expected the meadow at the top of the hill to be unchanged as well.

The meadow had been my place of solace during my teen years. I'd had a crush on the young landowner and my dreams of marrying him, building a large home with a big porch, having two children, and living happily ever after were my heart's desire. Unfortunately, David felt the six years of age that separated us was too much. While he would take me out on casual dates—as friends—his mind was set. The day he married another, part of me died.

Now, so many years later, a business conference brought me back. And since I had a rental car and time to kill before heading to the airport, I decided to drive to the cabin. I had planned to walk through the meadow and let the memories take their course, but as I made the last curve I couldn't believe what I saw. My meadow was gone! In its place were homes with front porches, sharp peaks, and shingled sides. I followed the signs offering homesites for sale, parked in front of the office, and walked inside.

He was older—more stooped—and a pair of wire-rimmed glasses perched on his nose. But I would have known that smile and those beautiful eyes anywhere. I stopped, uncertain if he would recognize me, and held my breath. And then his smile deepened and he pushed his glasses up on his head.

"Is it really you?" He asked as if he didn't believe it himself. "Carol? It's you isn't it?" When I didn't respond, he nodded. "Well, this is a first. I think you're speechless for the first time in your life."

Blinded by emotion, I shot a barrage of questions at him. "Where's the meadow? Who lives in these houses? What happened to the wildlife?" He couldn't stop chuckling as he walked toward me, his eyes tearing up.

"Where have you been?" He asked. "I've looked everywhere trying to find you. I wanted to talk about the plans for the meadow with you because I know it was a special place for you."

"But why?" I whispered. "Why did you do this, you didn't need the money."

"Ah, but I did." He motioned toward the door. "Do you have time today? I have something I need to show you."

I nodded, unable to speak.

"Let me take you for a ride in my chariot," he said as he opened the truck door for me and then walked to the other side and slipped in.

What surprise could he possibly have just for me, I wondered? I'd been gone for years.

He drove straight toward the mountaintop where we had spent so many days lying on our backs looking at the strolling clouds, chewing on freshly picked grass, and dreaming of life. The road was in better shape today, but still rutted and bumpy.

He glanced over at me apologetically. "Sorry about the bounce, I plan to have this graded next spring." Then with brows furrowed, he said, "I have asked so many people about you over the years, but no one knew where you had moved or what you were doing. And since you had married, I didn't know your last name. Then one day a line from a movie came to mind, you know the one: 'build it and she will come.'"

I look at him incredulously. "You looked for me? Why?"

He shrugged. "I made a mistake many years ago and I had hoped for another chance."

"You made a mistake? Fat chance! *You* with the perfect life all laid out? How could you have made a mistake?"

"You'll see. We're almost there."

As he made the last turn on the dirt road, a house came into view at the top of the hill. It had two stories with a railed porch on both levels. It was still under construction, but it was obvious that someone lived in it.

"Who lives here?" I asked, staring at the perfect home . . . the very home I had pictured as a teen.

"Well," he said slowly, "before I show you the house, I have something I have to tell you, Carol. I was wrong when I told you age made a difference. I realized that age doesn't matter if you both want the same thing." He pointed toward the house. "I built this for us, hoping one day you would find your way back. And," he added quickly, "if it's not too late, I have only one question for you."

"One question? After all these years, only one question?" My heart beat fast as I held to the hope that I was thinking of the same question he was, because I knew what answer I wanted to give.

My days of traveling to new and exotic places, looking for just the right niche, ended that day on the hill. ᑲ

The Town of Felton, California

Population: 4,700

History: A Woody Past

In 1843, Isaac Graham transferred his lumber mill from the Zayante land grant to the San Lorenzo River at Fall Creek. Some years later, Graham invested in a worthless silver mine and lost the lumber mill and the adjacent property to Edward Stanly. In 1868, Stanly envisioned the land he'd obtained from Graham as a future town and partitioned his property into bite-size plots, which he then sold to prospective settlers. He named the town after local educator and congressman, John Brooks Felton.

In the 1890s, Felton was primarily industrial. Surrounded by giant redwood trees, Felton's earliest residents reaped what they could from the lumber business. Additional industry included a paper mill, a powder works, and several lime kilns, which were in demand during World War I when lime for concrete was needed.

Prior to the arrival of the rail, teams of oxen were hitched to redwood log chains and slowly, yet steadily, redwood trunks were hauled out of the hills and forests. Logging was accelerated through the use of trains, and it wasn't long before the region's redwood-covered hills had been laid bare. By the early twentieth century, virtually every tree that could be cut and sold for a profit had been removed. These days, only a few select forests, including those at Big Basin, Henry Cowell Redwoods State Park, Fall Creek State Park, and the land where Graham located his camp, called Roaring Camp, remain unscathed. Long gone is the constant noise from saws and trains. Today, nearly 100 years later, Felton is a small bedroom community serving Santa Cruz and the Silicon Valley (San Jose, Santa Clara, Los Gatos, etc.). Many residents commute The Hill (Highway 17) to the Silicon Valley to work. ❧

Town Facts

First incorporated: Felton got its start in 1843.

Transportation: Bus is the most popular mode of transportation today, but forty years ago the train was the way to go. Nowadays, the railroad tracks are used only as a tourist attraction.

Location: Felton is located in Santa Cruz County, ninety-two miles south of San Francisco, between Ben Lomond and Santa Cruz, along Highway 9. Felton is five miles from the Pacific Ocean.

Places of note: The narrow-gauge railroad that runs from Felton to Bear Mountain is a current-day attraction, as is the Felton Covered Bridge, an old covered bridge located at Graham Hill and Covered Bridge roads and built in 1892. Felton's most historic and graceful building, originally the Presbyterian Church, was built in 1903. Since then, it has been home to the County Library. Henry Cowell State Park and Fall Creek State Park are additional places of note.

A Delight to Visit—Places of Interest

Roaring Camp—A narrow-gauge railroad takes passengers to the top of Bear Mountain on a beautiful ride through the redwood trees.

The Mount Hermon Christian Conference Center—Started in 1906, one of the finest Christian camps and conference centers in the country.

Henry Cowell State Park—The San Lorenzo River runs through the park, which has wonderful walking trails through the giant trees.

Fall Creek State Park—The Felton-area lime kilns can be found here; a great place to hike.

All-Star Washer Player

by Stephanie Ray Brown | *Clay, Kentucky*

AT TWELVE YEARS OLD, I was at a very awkward stage in life. I was no longer a little girl, but not quite a teenager. To make matters worse, I was chubby and coordination was not one of my strongest traits. On the other hand, my mother—and coach—was a very talented soft-ball player. Night after night I tried my best to impress her. Unfortunately, ballgame after ballgame I struck out. A good night for me would be hitting a fly ball to the pitcher. At times I felt like a terrible disappointment. I lacked my mother's athletic ability, and did not possess her love of the game.

One summer afternoon, my mother told us (my two brothers and me) that we were going to go visit Uncle David and Aunt Elsie. Since we lived in an apartment, going to the country was always a treat. I looked forward not only to running through the cornfield mazes and taking a dip in their small pond, but also to seeing Uncle David, whom I adored. Uncle David always had a way of making me feel special. This particular Saturday would be no exception.

When we arrived, he and my cousin Jeff were throwing metal rings at two holes in the ground. Curiosity got the best of me so I went over to watch. Dust flew in the air as Uncle David's metal ring sank into the hole.

"You win again," Jeff replied as he angrily marched past me.

When my uncle noticed me, he asked if I had ever played washers. Being a girl, my reply was that the only washers I knew were the ones that cleaned clothes. Chuckling, Uncle David explained that the metal rings were called washers. Picking the four washers off of the ground, he continued to explain his favorite game. When he was finished, he gave me the washers and offered tips on how to pitch better.

Later, as others gathered around, I moved out of the way to make room for the good players. But as they began to pair off, I was shocked to hear my uncle say he wanted me as his partner. I protested, saying I could not possibly play against anyone, but he insisted the only way to improve your skill was to actually play a game.

As the game progressed, I found myself not only enjoying but also wanting to win! We were beating everybody! Our winning was due to Uncle David's being one of the greatest washer players of all times—at least in the small town of Clay, Kentucky. To his twelve-year-old niece, he was a master at the game. The championship game was our team against my mother and older brother, Kevin.

Though I was extremely nervous, I somehow managed to pitch washer after washer until it was my last turn. As the washer went into the air and began to fall, I was amazed to see a cloud of dust appear as it sank into the hole. My first ringer! I had actually thrown the washer into the hole! Screaming and jumping up and down, I felt two strong arms lift me as Uncle David hugged me and whispered, "Way to go!"

Getting that ringer placed me on cloud nine for quite some time. In the months to come, this small success—especially sweet because I had beat my mother and brother—helped me gain back some of the self-confidence lost when I'd struggled on the softball field.

Although twenty-three summers have gone by since that day, I do not believe any of my other successes in life tasted as sweet. My mother has always told me that you never forget a person who was kind to you when you were a child, and I believe she's right. I will always remember how Uncle David raised my spirits as well as increasing my self-esteem that summer afternoon in his backyard. He made me feel like an all-star athlete.

Since then, during trying times I find myself dreaming about that country home, framed on each side by cornfields, which was the perfect place for an awkward preteen girl to get a great big boost of self-confidence. ᦉ

Can We Go Home Again?

by Gail Balden | *Dexter, Michigan*

AS I SIFT THROUGH MEMORIES of home and my childhood in the small town of Dexter, Michigan, during the '50s, I am reminded of buttons in my mother's button box. The memories seem so precious and sweet and are a reminder of what I'm made of. I can't help but wonder if we really can go home again. This question was reawakened recently when my friend Kandie asked me a startling question.

"When you die, do you want your ashes buried next to mine," she asked in a matter-of-fact tone.

"At Forest Lawn cemetery in Dexter?" I questioned in a puzzled voice.

"Of course," she replied with a laugh, "the cemetery near the millpond where we used to ice-skate."

As I pondered the idea, I thought how fitting it would be for us to end up together after all these years. I could imagine us settled in next to each other at Forest Lawn, near our parents, just like we were when we stayed overnight at each other's homes, just a stone's throw from each other.

"I walked by your old house the other day," she says, "and a woman was making up the bed on the porch. Remember when we slept out there on the Fourth of July? And how the sheets were always slightly damp and musty, the wool blanket on the bed scratchy?"

I remember. I remember when I first met Kandie in kindergarten in 1947 in the basement of Dexter Elementary School. We sat in small desks next to each other under the steam pipes attached to the furnace. Miss Mandegold was our teacher. She made us take a nap every afternoon. Along with the others, Kandie and I lay on rugs placed on the floor. Mine was braided, a rainbow of blues with long fringe on the ends that I fingered and stared at endlessly during nap time. Some of the time my mouth was taped shut while I was on the rug, maybe because I talked too much to Kandie, who was already my best friend. My report card was usually full of satisfactory checks except for one: "Whispers too much."

I'll never forget the big kindergarten trip Miss Mandegold scheduled. It was a train ride to Ann Arbor—our first outing! Unfortunately, I got the measles and couldn't go. I cried so hard I could barely see Kandie and the class as they walked by my house on their way to the train depot.

As the years rolled on, Kandie and I played, skipped, and roller-skated through life. We saw movies—like *Singing in the Rain*—for a quarter at the Dexter Theater. Then we came home and acted the movie out by dancing in puddles with our umbrellas. We had Halloween parties and haunted houses. It makes me laugh to remember how long it took us to figure out why Kandie's mother insisted we call it a haunted house and not a "horror" house. We anxiously awaited snow days so we could take our Flexible Flyers down Hoey's Hill, and then stay up most of the night discussing our first crushes. We learned to drive a stick shift in her yellow 1952 Chevy, clunking and jerking about town laughing so hard we could barely see. While practicing parallel parking, I ran over my parents' garbage can and it got stuck under the wheels, which brought on another chorus of laughter.

Dexter was our town. I guess it still is. Almost every Saturday morning in summer, we packed a lunch and took our bikes to Huron River Park, pedaling across the green steel bridge next to her grandfather's cider mill. In the fall, the cider mill was where we hung out, watching them grind the apples and waiting to sample the frothy juice. It was here, on the banks of the Huron River, that Kandie and I first tried fly-fishing. We never caught anything edible, as our lines were usually caught on the bushes behind us.

Eventually we went off to college, jobs, marriage, motherhood, and divorce.

Life has a way of breaking a person open, and Kandie and I had our fair share of pain and sadness. Over the years, we often ran back to each other seeking comfort and solace in each other's love. For class reunions, Kandie and I came from opposite coasts. We met early and stayed late; we laughed, we cried, we remembered. We drove around town looking at our old haunts, bowled at the bowling alley where we used to set pins, and picked up where we left off on our last visit.

Now, after fifteen years in New York City, Kandie has moved back to Dexter, to her home on Main Street. I like the idea. Now that my childhood home where I lived for twenty-five years belongs to someone else and I won't see my father working in his rose garden anymore, I am comforted by the thought that Kandie is there, just a block away in her house on Main Street.

On my last visit I noticed the deep purple lilacs, which continue to bloom over my old garage, and was comforted that someone was picking them for bouquets. Someone was hanging sheets on the line in the backyard—sheets for the bed on the front porch.

The three red maples our sixth-grade class planted on Arbor Day, fifty years ago, remain strong and tall in front of Dexter Elementary School, and our favorite hangout, the A & W Root Beer, still stands at the edge of town, just past the millpond. Carhops still take our orders, and every Tuesday—rain or shine—is Coney Dog day.

Can you really go home again? For Kandie and me the answer is yes.

Perhaps someday another pair of dear friends will walk through the cemetery arm in arm on their way to someplace else, and stop for a moment to contemplate the inscription on our gravestone: "Kandie Kay Waggoner and Gail Barbara Frank, friends forever." ∽

Uncle Ben

by Jamie Cope | *Racine, Ohio*

I SAT IN AUNT HELEN'S LIVING ROOM studying the pictures of my uncle Ben that seemed to bring life to every corner of her house. In many of the pictures he looked so young I hardly recognized him, but then I saw one that was "my" Uncle Ben. It made me remember a special time, several years ago and a few miles down the road.

I don't remember how old I was, probably around twelve, but I do remember it was summer and it was hot. Like many hot summer days, this one was spent with my brother, Todd, and two favorite cousins, Randy and David. David was the oldest, but didn't seem to mind hanging out with the rest of us. Maybe because we looked up to him so much, at least I did. Todd was a couple of years younger than David, and I was a couple of years younger than Todd. We hardly ever fought, but we both knew who would win if we did. We also knew who would win when we played chess, and it wasn't me. Randy was just a few months younger than I was, so we kinda shared the "baby" status of the group.

I can't imagine any four boys who could get along as well as we did. There were scuffles and an occasional wrestling match broke out, but it always ended with us closer than when we started. We were all best friends.

Hot summer days would find us exploring, slaying dragons, imitating our favorite sports heroes, or just skipping rocks. On this particular day we were visiting our aunt Helen and uncle Ben at their farm in Racine, Ohio. We really didn't know much about Aunt Helen or Uncle Ben. They lived on a farm, so they must be farmers. It wasn't that we never saw them. We saw them probably three or four times a year. It's just that our conversations never got past, "How's school?" or "Nice weather we're having, isn't it?"

We started the day playing in the barn on tall stacks of hay. That's the day I learned that heat goes up. Both heat and wasps were good motivators to find something else to do, but before we could find another adventure, in walked Uncle Ben with some fishing rods. Well, a couple of them were actually store-bought rods like I was used to seeing, but others were cane poles with fishing line tied to the ends. As we prepared to go fishing, digging worms and gathering hooks, Uncle Ben's excitement was obvious. He wasn't excited about taking us fishing. He was excited about fishing. He was a big kid with a magical parental supervision certificate sown into his pocket. He was one of us.

He led us through the cow pastures, carefully avoiding the electrical fences, to a shaded area of a large creek. After some minor fussing about who would use the cane poles and who would use the other rods, we were fishing. I never considered myself a good fisherman, and that day was no different. It helped that no one else was getting a nibble. Then I got a big strike! I was going to be the only one to catch a fish, and it was going to be huge! After a struggle that probably lasted at least half a minute, I reeled in a nice-size bass.

I was up on the bank holding out my rod and wondering what to do next when Uncle Ben climbed down to unhook my fish. I was really starting to like that guy! But when he touched the fish, it flopped right out of his hands and into the water. As the splash settled, I looked up at Uncle Ben. He seemed more upset than I was.

Bending over, he told me to kick him right in the seat of his pants. This was something new to me, and I thought, "It must be a farmer thing," and started to laugh. I can't remember if anyone else caught a fish that day, but I know none of them got the chance to kick Uncle Ben. ⬥

A Plank Is the Deed to My Memories

by Polly Camp Kreitz | *Munford, Alabama*

RETURNING TO MY CHILDHOOD HOME for a final goodbye brought a flood of bittersweet tears.

Munford, Alabama, located halfway between the county seats of Talladega and Anniston, was home to about 700 citizens back in the '40s. Now, years later, as I passed through town, a swirl of memories enveloped me. I would never forget my grandfather's grocery store, the post office, Dr. Harris's drugstore, the gas station, Carter's Hardware, or Aunt Hattie, the woman who lived back in the mountains and ran a still, selling moonshine in pint jars. Munford was a typical small town, but it was also special, and I would miss it dearly, especially my home.

As I stepped into the bedroom of my growing-up years, vivid memories erupted and my eyes lingered on the small fireplace. On cold winter mornings my father came in to build the fire. When the logs were blazing, he would gently touch my shoulder and say, "Time to get up." As he slowly raised the two window shades at the head of my bed, he always added, "God's given us another beautiful day."

The memory of his soft voice and me looking up into his blue eyes still seems so real, even after all these years. I remember snuggling back under the warm quilts my mother had made and mumbling, "Just a little longer."

Every morning, Father rose early and warmed up the house. The first fire he lit was the woodstove so Mother could begin preparing meals. The sound of the oven opening and closing was enough to get me dressed and to the table in record time. In my opinion, the perfect way to begin any day was with hot buttered biscuits.

In the evening, we popped fluffy white popcorn in a wire basket over the coals in the living room fireplace. There was no need for conversation. The closeness we shared filled us with love.

Crossing to the front porch, through a door in my bedroom, I sat down in the old glider and gently swayed back and forth. Today I faced two losses. Though there was still a sparkle in Father's eyes—as if he held a secret—and an occasional faint smile crept across his face, his illness was slowly draining him. The second loss was this house. It had been our home for as long as I could remember. Now it belonged to another family.

Unwilling to close this chapter in my life just yet, I let myself be hypnotized by the steady rhythmic squeaks of the glider. It felt so good to be home. Closing my eyes, I let summers from long ago crowd in, hot and sultry. At dusk, lightning bugs put on a show that captivated my brother, sister, and I. We each had a Mason jar with holes punched in the lid to use as a lightning-bug lantern. Always competing, we eventually ended up on the porch watching the moon dart in and out of the clouds, casting dark shadows through the grove of trees in the nearby cemetery.

Summertime was filled with remembrances of so many tastes—ripe watermelon or muskmelon brought from the field in early morning, still cooled by the droplets of dew, or a bucket of fresh-picked blackberries made into a cobbler. And how eager we were to sample the fresh honey from the hives in our grandfather's apple orchard, and chew on the waxy honeycomb. But perhaps our old, wooden, hand-cranked ice cream maker served up the best treat. Each member of our family got to take a turn at the crank. The one lucky enough to be turning it when the ice cream hardened got the prize—the paddle! The first lick of ice cream clinging to the paddle was always the best.

Torrid, humid heat often broke into afternoon thunderstorms and rain hit the tin roof of our house in a riot of sound, while cool breezes wafted through the open windows bringing welcome relief. The steady rhythm of raindrops had a lulling effect on us as we sprawled across the bed to listen. Dotted swiss curtains swayed like dancers over our heads in the breezes.

Opening my tear-filled eyes I took one last look at my childhood home, a home built from love. My parents drew up the floor plans on a piece of brown wrapping paper from my grandfather's grocery store. A long room on one side of the house was like a glass observatory. During the four seasons, a kaleidoscope of changing colors rippled across the horizon as far as the eye could see. Field stones gathered from the hillside, each handpicked by my mother for its beauty in shape and color, were used to create the fireplace that dominated one entire wall. Mother was right when she said a fireplace was the heartbeat of a home. I'll always treasure the memory I have of my father sitting nearby each evening in his favorite chair for his daily Bible reading.

I come from people who believe the home place is as vital and necessary as the air we breathe. To us, home is where the sense of family is preserved and where a Bible is the most prominent book in each room.

Today, piles of sawdust surround the corroded equipment at the now-idle sawmill, and a rusted Allis Chambers tractor, hidden by overgrown weeds, stands alone by the pond. I look around once more, my eyes drinking it all in. All of these things are what created my family history. History I am not entirely able to leave behind, as evidenced by the twelve-inch piece of weathered plank cut from the side of an old barn that boards the plane back to Texas with me. This plank is my real estate, the deed to my memories. It's a part of me as surely as I am a part of it. ⌒

The Grape Jelly Lady

by Marcia E. Brown | *Muskogee, Oklahoma*

ON THE RARE OCCASIONS when I return to visit my childhood hometown of Muskogee, Oklahoma, I slow the car as much as the law allows.

Each of the half-dozen visits over the past fifty years has triggered sharp memories—some sad, some happy. There is sadness in my heart when I remember loved ones now gone, and also when I see that my hometown is changing, but my heart leaps joyfully at the sight of the remaining familiar landmarks. Downtown has lost the fine marble building where my grandfather had his dental office, and more than thirty years ago our street with its large Victorian homes—set back among gardens and a sidewalk of hexagonal concrete blocks where I once played hopscotch—was demolished to make room for a highway.

But old sycamores remain nearby, still dropping leaves for children to scuff. Our old church remains active. And most of the old neighborhoods still offer a slower, quieter lifestyle unknown to city dwellers.

As I drive slowly into town, I hear a train a few blocks away. Not the old, soot-spouting engines we knew in my childhood, but the modern whistle echoes a little of the past and I think of my grandmother, who was known as the Grape Jelly Lady.

During the Great Depression, three generations of our family shared my maternal grandparents' spacious house on that lost street that was graced by a canopy of elms. Pop-Pop—my name for my grandfather—had been a respected community leader and loving family patriarch since he and Grandma settled in Muskogee in 1900. When times grew hard in the 1930s, my father and uncle were often out of work. Pop-Pop and Grandma made us welcome. We all pitched in, Mama and I helping Grandma around the house, and Dad and my uncle doing the outdoor chores on the half-acre lot.

Our home was halfway between downtown Muskogee and the place along the railroad tracks where trains slowed or stopped as they approached the station. This was a favorite spot for tramps riding the rails to hop on or off a train. Of the thousands upon thousands of out-of-work men passing through Oklahoma this way, dozens every week jumped from the trains and walked into town to look for work and food. Our street was a major thoroughfare for these unfortunate souls.

Scarcely a day passed without at least one of these transient men knocking on our back door to beg for work or food or both. Many were too weak from hunger and exposure to do much work, but Grandma never turned anyone away no matter how bad things might be within our own family.

After a while, Mama noticed that sometimes beggars passed by other houses along our street yet always knocked at Grandma's back door. Naturally, we began to wonder why our house was such a consistent target. We got our answer one morning when Grandma's cupboards and ice box were nearly empty and a gray-haired man in tattered clothes—black with coal dust from the trains—knocked on the kitchen door. Because we'd had a meager breakfast ourselves, Grandma hesitated before opening the door.

The man before her was pitiful and emaciated. With trembling hands he took off an old fedora and held it respectfully. "Lady, I haven't eaten in three days," he said in a cracked voice. "Please, can you help me?"

Grandma was distressed. Her usual offering for these sad wayfarers was strong coffee, two or three fried eggs, bacon, and several slices of toast liberally spread with her homemade grape jelly.

With rare tears in her eyes, she answered, "I'm sorry. This morning I don't have anything. I don't know if I can even give my family lunch."

"Don't you *even have any bread and grape jelly?*" the man at the door pleaded.

"No. All I can give you today is a cup of coffee and a few crackers."

Then Grandma looked sharply at him and demanded, "How do you know I usually have grape jelly?"

"Oh, your house is marked, ma'am. Everybody riding the rails knows you never turn anybody away. You're the Grape Jelly Lady," he answered, grinning shyly.

Though Grandma and Mama searched, they never found the tramps' mark. Grandma was flattered, for she loved people and lived her life by the philosophy expressed in her favorite lines of poetry: "Let me live in my house by the side of the road and be a friend to man." Sam Walter Foss might have written his poem "The House by the Side of the Road" just for her.

"Don't we even have any grape jelly?" became a standard joke in our family whenever the household ran short of anything.

On a visit today in this new century, I look down the empty space that was once our street. In my mind I still see the elm trees and lawns, the streets and homes, and a shabby figure trudging along searching for a secret mark and, upon finding it, quickening his steps toward the house of the Grape Jelly Lady. ∾

A Promise

by Steven Manchester | *Westport, Massachusetts*

I WAS NINE YEARS OLD when I walked into Mrs. Parson's fourth-grade classroom, in Westport, Massachusetts, and fell head over heels in love. She was a heavy-set woman with kind eyes and a raspy voice, and from the moment she looked at me there was no doubt that she cared very deeply. She was the perfect teacher.

She always listened with concern and was quick with praise or encouragement. "What a wonderful poem," she'd whisper, or, "I know someday you'll make me very proud!" And God, how I wanted to! It was midyear when I learned that the saintly woman was equally quick with the truth. It was the greatest lesson I could have ever learned.

I was walking home from school when I spotted three neighborhood bullies waiting for me. The Benoit brothers were frighteningly tough, but nothing compared to their Amazon sister, who'd worn a cast on her right arm for as long as I could remember. My nemesis, Danny Benoit, was swollen with the courage provided by his cheering siblings. He approached and, without a word, threw one shot at me before his brother and sister jumped in. As the

Benoits pounced and inflicted their damage, I went down and curled up into the fetal position.

Bleeding and ashamed, I returned home to hide my battle scars.

As the weeks rolled by, the thought of the Benoits loomed over me like a five-ton anvil. The memory of the unanswered beating hurt much more than the lingering cuts and bruises.

Not too long after my initial beating, we were at morning recess when Danny Benoit approached, grinning. He was alone, but that didn't stop me from trembling. It was time to redeem my honor, and I knew it. "Ready for another beatin'?" he barked, loud enough to ensure my public humiliation. I swallowed hard and remember being amazed at how small the world suddenly became. Even though a circle of spectators joyously awaited the blood sport, as far as I was concerned, it was only Danny Benoit and me. Everything else was darkness.

Danny started with name-calling. I followed suit. Danny threatened. I matched each vulgar word. My knees quivered and a string of sweat beads formed across my forehead. Everything seemed to be happening in slow motion. I could hear my heart beating hard in my ears. My breathing was quick, and, if only for the sake of saving face, I knew I wasn't going to cower. While our peers cheered us on, I felt the urge to vomit. It was a living nightmare. Danny was still grinning. I just couldn't take it anymore. As the crowd began to chant, panic made me lunge.

There was a brief scuffle and in one strange, syrupy moment, I had Danny on the ground. To my surprise, I'd pinned my enemy! Danny stared back at me with fright in his eyes. But at that moment all that registered was that I was on top. With his arms pinned behind him, I went to work. I ignored his pleas for mercy. I had to prove that I was a man.

I never let up until I realized Mrs. Parson was trying to pull us apart. I let go right away then and heard the crowd erupt into cheers. It was a victory for anyone who had ever feared Danny Benoit. Everyone celebrated, except Mrs. Parson. Instead, she grabbed my ear and forced me to look down at Danny, who by now had folded into the fetal position and was crying.

"I hope you're proud of yourself, Mr. Manchester," she hissed.

Emotions churned inside me. In confusion, I looked up at her and crumpled. The disappointment on her face broke my heart in two. I'd never felt so awful in my whole life. She shook her head, disgustedly. "I thought you were better than this. I really thought you were a bigger person than this."

At that moment, something inside of me died. Even as I was escorted to the vice principal's office where I received strict punishment, Mrs. Parson's face loomed before my eyes. Then I suffered my parents' wrath. Multiplied a thousand times, neither of these punishments could have ever compared to the pain I suffered from looking into Mrs. Parson's disappointed face. I'd let her down. In turn, I'd let myself down.

Days later, when I'd finally drummed up enough courage to approach Mrs. Parson, I promised her I would never disappoint her again.

"I'm sorry for what I did, but I am a bigger person," I explained solemnly. "I am the person you thought I was. I'm going to prove it." With a simple nod, she accepted my apologetic vow and watched me walk back to my desk.

Though I had to avoid several potential fights, the remainder of my fourth-grade year passed without further trouble. On our last day of school, Mrs. Parson gave me a hug and whispered, "I expect big things from you, so don't let either of us down, okay?"

With tearful eyes, I nodded.

I'm now thirty-five years old, Mrs. Parson has long since retired, and my life's path has brought me back home to Westport. There's not a day that goes by, though, that I don't honor the promise I made to her. Because of the person she was, I've become who I am, and I'm eternally grateful.

Home Again

by Bob Rose | *Lingle, Wyoming*

I GREW UP IN AN IDYLLIC TIME, just after World War II. The postwar economy brought prosperity. Families boomed, and technology kept improving our creature comforts. To make things even better, I lived in the tiny town of Lingle, Wyoming, population: 450. There, kids rode their bicycles to the playground or the ball field, and parents didn't need to fret over their welfare. On Sunday mornings, the carillon call from the local church called folks to worship. Neighbors chatted, even in the absence of back fences.

In the summer, folks shared the bounty of their gardens, and in the winter you didn't stop shoveling snow at your own property line. If sickness or death visited a household, the whole community turned out to help with meals carried in and services offered. Life centered around school, church, and Sunday dinners at Marge's Lingle Café. On Veterans' Day and Memorial Day, the veterans all turned out in their old uniforms, and the whole town paid homage to those who had so greatly served our nation in time of war.

As I barged through adolescence, television brought images of a different world—one filled with great adventure and opportunity.

I could scarcely wait for high school graduation so I could leave Lingle and venture into life in the *real* world. I attended the state university, where I had the opportunity to tour Europe twice with singing groups. I spent time in New York City and Denver, and seldom thought of Lingle.

After I married, I lived in various parts of Wyoming, until I again heard the call to venture out into the Great Beyond. I took my family to Texas, where we lived first on the border, in Brownsville, and then in its heart, just outside of Austin. We enjoyed the abundance of goods and services available within driving distance, and the things that a large population base afforded, but we missed the personality of home. We tired of living next to strangers, and having no one care about us, or us about them. We hated the traffic jams and the rude attitude that frequently arises from unfamiliarity.

Three years ago, we came home. Job availability kept us out of Lingle, but instead led us to Sinclair, Wyoming, also populated by about 450 folks. This little town, originally built as a company town for a large petroleum refinery, mirrors all the attributes I longed for as I remembered Lingle. It sits just off of Interstate 80, and boasts a hotel twice patronized by Amelia Earhart. However, the hotel stopped serving guests years ago, and few travelers now detour through town in their haste to reach other destinations.

Still, tree-lined streets give access to houses reflective of a different time. Our seventy-five-year-old house looks much as it did when first built, with its broad front porch welcoming folks to stop by. Kids ride their bicycles all over town with no fear of abduction, a walk with the dog includes several genial conversations along the way, senior citizens gather every Wednesday morning at the town hall for coffee and donuts.

Folks here remember birthdays and anniversaries. They speak at the post office and at the town hall. When one has a need, plenty offer help—and all without being asked. On Sunday mornings, the church bell tolls, calling folks to worship. Inside, Jesus shepherds his lambs from the lone stained-glass window at the front. Songs raise praise to accompaniment played on the old, original, upright piano, and the sermon notes rest on a pulpit hand-carved more than fifty years before.

We don't have any shopping here, but we are all used to driving to get things we need and are adept at buying for future need instead of just for the immediate. The world rushes by in so many ways, but life in Wyoming seems caught in a time warp. It's peaceful and friendly. And when, in spite of its similarities, I still find myself longing to walk the streets of the original, I can drive a scant (by Wyoming standards) 200 miles to Lingle.

They call Marge's Lingle Café the Stagecoach Inn now, but other than that, nothing has really changed in Lingle. The food and friendliness remain the same, and the carillon still sounds on Sundays. Mom and Dad rest in peace on the hill east of town, near Grandpa and Grandma, and folks still know who I am. They don't treat me like a visitor, either. They know Lingle will always be my hometown. ⁓

The Town of Lingle, Wyoming

Population: 510

Early History Remains Important

The famous Oregon, Mormon, and Texas trails follow the Platte River and travel right through Lingle—some of the wagon train ruts are still visible.

The Grattan Massacre site is three miles southwest of Lingle.

Old Fort Laramie is roughly fifteen miles southwest of Lingle.

Several large irrigation canals, which were among the earliest in this part of the country, remain in use today.

Town History

Lingle was named for Hiram D. Lingle, who owned much of the surrounding land. In 1903, he married Elizabeth Lee Rider. On their honeymoon, they became interested in developing irrigation in the Goshen County area. When in 1918 a small town started to spring up south of the Lingle ranch, close to the railroad tracks, it seemed only natural that the town be named Lingle in commemoration of Mr. Lingle's services in developing the territory.

Town Facts

First incorporated: September 1918

Transportation: Resources today are the railroad for freight, and private auto for people. Public transportation is extremely limited. The nearest small airport is forty-five miles east at Scottsbluff, Nebraska, but most people drive the 200 miles to Denver to get a better fare. Bus service is a similar situation, with very limited local access. Cheyenne is the closest bus stop for Greyhound or Trailways.

Location: Lingle lies roughly 95 miles northwest of Cheyenne, Wyoming, 195 miles north of Denver, and 200 miles southwest of Rapid City, South Dakota. Casper is 135 miles northwest of Lingle, and Fort Laramie is 10 miles west.

Original name: Lingle is said by some to be a continuation of the town of Wyncote. When the town of Wyncote failed to prosper, many of its buildings and businesses were moved three miles down the road to Lingle.

From Local Fame to the Silver Screen

Jerry Hill, a local resident, played pro football for the Baltimore Colts in the 1960s.

Jimmy Stewart and Carol Baker stopped in town and imbibed after a day of filming the movie *Cheyenne Autumn* in nearby Ft. Laramie.

Johnny Cash once stopped in town for a visit while on tour.

Changing Hearths

by Annemarieke Tazelaar | *Saugatuck, Michigan*

I GAZED AT THE STATUE OF LIBERTY IN AWE. From the spikes on her crown all the way to her feet, she personified everything that I had heard about America—big. As our tiny ship bobbed on the wake of cargo carriers and harbor boats heading toward an area of idle luxury liners, my father shielded us from the cold February wind with one arm, and with the other pointed to buildings that reached to the sky.

"Home," he said, with tears in his voice. "We're home!" My brothers and I exchanged a look. Would Grandmother's cottage be tall, like the buildings of New York? To me, home was much different. It was our bomb-damaged house in the Netherlands. Though the roof leaked, the only working faucet was outside, and rat traps were full each morning, I had my own room and my friends and I knew all the magical places in the neighborhood that were still intact.

For a few months, home had been a garage where we slept on straw with the scurrying mice. In the evenings, by the light of a bare bulb, Mother read to us. Each day we gathered the eggs left in the outhouse by the owner's chicken. When Mother had enough she made an omelet fortified with mushrooms foraged from the forest. Often, during the war, home had been the cozy living room of my Dutch grandparents' home, Grandfather dozing in his favorite chair, his beret askew on his bald head, and Grandmother carrying a tray of afternoon tea and cookies. Home was the chime of their small French clock, the feel of a soft Persian rug beneath my feet.

When my father left Saugatuck, Michigan, in 1931 to work in the Netherlands, he had no idea it would be fifteen years before he would return. He met my mother in Arnhem. Two houses and two babies later, their roots were well established in a new neighborhood with other young families. Illness or other circumstances postponed his return trip, and by 1939, booking passage on a ship became impossible.

Four days after the United States entered the war, Father was arrested and sent to a German prison for American civilians. Through letters, we learned that our family could participate in a prisoner exchange, and Father's dream of going home was rekindled. But, though Father was released from prison, the ship scheduled to transport us never returned from New York. A few years later, when Arnhem was besieged by a fierce battle, we trekked to a northern province where we lived until the end of the war. When we returned to Arnhem, rain-soaked debris lay rotting in bombed-out, abandoned buildings, and Father resumed his quest to return to Michigan. This time, passport pictures were taken, household goods were crated, and, finally, we boarded a cattle ship that had been converted into a passenger transport.

After waiting for several hours in the harbor, we were escorted into the reception room of an immigration building. We sat across from a woman with nails painted red and eyes outlined in black—a real American lady.

Everything was new. We saw our very first movie, though I was unable to understand why people around me laughed so hard as two men, one short and fat and the other tall and skinny, bounced and ran and fell while trying to save another painted American lady, called the Gypsy Girl.

When Father gave us each a stick of chewing gum, informing us to chew it but not to swallow it, I was mystified and a little afraid. I couldn't swallow it? Did that mean I'd have to keep it in my mouth for the rest of my life?

We watched in awe as American skaters in beautiful trim clothes skimmed across the ice in Rockefeller Center, their skate blades springing from their shoes. In Holland, our skates had been strapped onto our boots.

Meanwhile, Father grew more and more anxious. He promised that very soon he would introduce us to his mother and sisters and take us to his favorite fishing holes on the Saugatuck River. We'd attend church picnics, eat a huge fruit called watermelon, and swim in Lake Michigan. I would go to a new school and have American friends, and, he assured me, a beautiful doll awaited me on my bed at Grandma's cottage.

As our train from New York neared the Saugatuck depot, Father peered out of the smudged window, then suddenly waved vigorously at a group of people who watched the train cars. "There they are!"

They waved back, yelling, "Lester! It's Lester!"

We pressed our noses to the glass as Father pointed. "That's Grandma! And your aunts, Hattie, Jo, Emma. There's Uncle Ben."

With arms outstretched, Father's tall, lanky form leaped out of the railcar and rushed toward an elderly woman. Her companions stayed back as Father folded his mother into his arms. We, too, stood poised by the door, as all watched this long-anticipated moment.

"My boy," Grandma sobbed. "You're back!" She held him at arm's length and looked at his face, then at us. "And Nel . . . the children . . . my little ones." And as if a dam broke, a sea of people floated toward us and I became engulfed in fur coat embraces and perfumed kisses. Though Father's enthusiasm was contagious, I clung to Mother's hand for safety.

As Father drove Aunt Hattie's black Ford to the cottage, he laughed with delight. "I haven't been behind the wheel of a car since before the war. But I still know the way." From photographs and my father's many stories, I recognized the boxy wooden house and huge porch as we drew near.

"There it is," Father said, his voice choking, "just like I remember it. The chestnut tree is bigger, and the boat by the dock . . . the Dodo? Nel, you will love the view of the river from upstairs!"

When we were all out of the car, Father put his arm around my mother's waist, and I saw tears in his eyes as they walked toward his childhood home. ᧁᴗ

The Ditch Rider

by Lois Larrance Requist | *Nampa, Idaho*

LEAVING CALIFORNIA ON INTERSTATE 80, I pass by the bright lights of Reno and eventually arrive in Winnemucca, turn north on Highway 95, and drive through Nevada and one corner of Oregon. As I drive through Jordan Valley it reminds me of my Idaho roots, the farmland flat and placid in every direction around the small town.

The pull of childhood increases as I pass the WELCOME TO IDAHO sign and wind through the mountains and finally see the valley where I was raised, spread out ahead. My hometown: Nampa. A sense of returning to the soil and the water that feeds it pervades as I cross the bridge in Marsing. Then I remember the ditch rider.

In 1946, Idaho's Boise Valley hummed with growth. As a curious seven-year-old, I loved to climb the cottonwood trees alongside of our house to stare across the vast land of fields and farms. The air was abuzz with insects. Near each farmhouse was a barn, sometimes a granary, a chicken house, a stack of hay, a tractor with a plow attached. The smell of hay and manure mixed with dust from the dirt road in front of our house. About six o'clock each morning and evening, farmers guided cows into barns for feeding and milking, pouring buckets of the white liquid through a strainer into the cans that would go to the creamery.

By nature, this land is a desert, but huge irrigation projects have changed it. Every spring, starting about mid-April, the control wheels at Arrow Rock and Lucky Peak Dam begin letting out the water that floods and feeds the land. It flows from the Boise River into various canals, directed through ever-smaller channels to reach each farm.

With the water came the ditch rider. I never knew his name, but when my mother mentioned spotting his presence, she did so in a soft, quiet way and her face was solemn.

No matter the technology of the system, it also depended upon humans. Each farm had assigned watering times, which, if violated, caused disruption. If a farmer went to irrigate and found there was no water, or very little, a search for the water began. The ditch rider was needed. In his watery domain, the ditch rider hovered at the edge of our lives, never quite belonging, always in charge. Because he was seen in only one way, he took on larger-than-life proportions. Shortly after his arrival, the brown earth turned green and yellow, trees and flowers came to life, our lilac bush blossomed, and the peony buds swelled.

All day, the ditch rider drove the dirt roads, looking at and beyond us. The blue of his eyes was a part of the landscape. The sun seared his skin. I thought that the sky and the land must be imprinted on his mind.

His job was to keep the water flowing. In the 100-degree weather of summer, a few hours or days without water and the bur- geoning life would begin to shrivel. He probably spent many hours shoveling mud out of culverts and cursing the dirt that forever flew in his face, but I never saw him that way. When he stopped to talk to a tractor driver or in front of one of the houses along our road, everyone quit what they were doing and watched as he picked a stalk of long grass, tore off the outer leaves, and began chewing it. He didn't say much, but even the surliest and most independent farmer listened to his words.

Once the crops were harvested, the water was turned off. Yellow, orange, and red leaves fell all over the yard and the ditch rider drove away in his pickup truck, one arm resting where the window would be if it were rolled up. It never was. ∽

Circles of Fire

by Margaret A. Frey | *Burlington Township, New Jersey*

I FLEW HOME FOR A WEEK, rented a car, and zigzagged through heavy traffic along Route 295. As I drove, I passed old, familiar landmarks—signs for the Cherry Hill Mall where I'd spent too much money and time as a girl, and the battle-gray bulwark of the naval station, humped like a beached whale, outside Mt. Holly, New Jersey. It whisked past as I headed for Burlington Township, a few miles north.

I'd come to help my sister, Kat, with last-minute details before selling the family house. It was a sad but necessary task. Our father's health had failed. Over fifty years of living had already been sold, traded, and given away, and now the remains were loaded into a for-lorn-looking dump truck. Chairs, rugs, and assorted bric-a-brac were stacked like so much kindling, by men we had never seen before and were unlikely to see again.

The job nearly done, I walked outside. Oak and sugar maple leaves carpeted the front yard, and the woody smells of October were thick and pungent. I closed my eyes. With little effort, I traveled back in time.

◄◦►

241

Childhood autumns commenced shortly after school started. Farmers' fields turned pale and brittle while treetops stroked the sky with orange and red. Squirrels hoarded, geese honked, and the annual leaf burns began. Air pollution standards and fire laws would later slam a lid on the practice. Bad for the lungs, the authorities insisted. A danger to small children, and for God's sake, the awful stink! But memories survive regulation and thin-lipped opinion.

"Whatever goes up, must come down," Pop said, rake tines rattling. Pop was a dedicated composter long before the organic farming fad. Nothing fancy, mind you. A simple chicken-wire hoop proved adequate, loaded with leaves and vegetable scraps. A daily turning guaranteed a thick, dark dressing, a goopy treat for the trees and shrubs. Neighbors thought the idea crazed and equally smelly, but Pop's lush spring flowerbeds countered all debate.

By early October, lawns humped with waves of brilliant color. Gentle swells at first, the mounds grew in proportion to the stripped down branches while the streets were transformed into narrow, leaf-lined chutes. As youngsters, we knew the piles were off-limits, but anyone with a bike yearned to ride the tunnels, kick the mounds, hoot and shriek as leaves flew off a knee or gloriously spewed with a defiant kick. We were warned about burrowing, told of children mangled by careless delivery vans or smothered in the leafy duff. Fueled by restless energy, we turned careless ears to grim warnings and caution. We were flat out nonbelievers in danger and death.

The burnings started before the north wind shifted. The Midnight Express, Pop called it, when the blowing resembles a freight train's howl. Neighborhood men gathered early on the weekends, denim collars flipped up. With good-natured shouts and joking, they raked out staggered leaf piles, then carefully set and stoked the fires like blue-collared priests.

Temperatures nose-dived. The week following Halloween the trees clicked and rattled. The final burn attracted spectators, who, bundled in coats and scarves, stomped their feet and breathed long, white plumes. Brown-bagged bottles were passed among the adults, hot cocoa for the rest. Laughter erupted, but the mood settled down to somber when the last of summer whooshed into twilight. Daylight was short now, slanting to a pearly gray.

The fires blazed then dwindled to embers, but the circles of fire remained branded on the streets. The scorch marks disappeared quietly beneath a rush of early snow and lavish turkey feasts.

Pop said the fires were an ancient tradition and ensured the growing season's return. My friends scoffed at the notion of fire charms. The burnings were an efficient disposal of year-end litter, they said. Cheap and easy, nothing more.

My sister tapped me on the shoulder, interrupting my thoughts. "You okay?"

I shrugged off a chill and smiled.

"Well, that's it," she said. "That's the last of it." We watched the rig choke and wobble down the street. Kat locked the front door. "Strange isn't it? All those years in this house. Cleared out for good now. Never thought I'd see the day." She sighed. "You coming back to my place? I'll fix some lunch. Then we can swing over to Voorhees and visit Pop. The doctors say he's doing better."

I nodded. "You go on. I'll be along in a minute."

Kat backed her car out with a quick wave and the traditional honk we gave as excitable young women whenever leaving the house. I watched her round the corner and then stood facing the empty two-story colonial. The picture windows were the same ones Kat and I had decorated each holiday, where Pop proudly erected the annual blue spruce, our mother fretted over custom-made draperies, and wild birds smacked themselves silly against the clear glass every spring. It was difficult to imagine the house belonging to strangers, people with different faces and names and ways of doing things.

Chimney smoke came from somewhere down the street and my mind moved back to leaf burns and rake tines.

Here's a secret even Kat doesn't know. I burn leaves every autumn. I contain the blazes in metal drums to avoid citations and angry complaints. The smoke puffs and curls across my patio, and my breath blows white while I stomp the chill from my bones. Maybe the tradition is mere superstition, an Old World story recycled from the ancient past. But I continue, in my own way, a small tribute to my father, the neighborhood, and all the customs and dusty stories that came before. It's a small thing, but I cannot let it go. The ritual works like magic, you see. Without fail, it brings the summer back.

One final look, then I scrambled into my car. Halfway down the street, I honked my horn and smiled. The house was behind me now, but there were many seasons of remembering still ahead.

A Prayer for My Brother

by Cindy Robert | *Redford Township, Michigan*

I GREW UP IN REDFORD TOWNSHIP, a small suburb in Michigan. It was at a time and a place where nothing seemed to change except the seasons. At least until I was eight and my brother left home.

With an eleven-year age difference, I didn't really think this would have a large impact on my life. I was more interested in when my sister, who was nine years older then me, would be going so I could have the bedroom to myself.

Even being as self-absorbed as I was, I couldn't help but notice some changes in our home. My sister, whose main goal in life was to provoke me, actually started being nice. Mom, who seldom cried, now frequently burst into tears. Dad, Mr. Don't-Sit-So-Close-to-the-Television, now spent his free time glued just inches from it. He never watched anything fun anymore—like the four o'clock movie or cartoons—it was always the news. Thinking the news had to be fascinating, one day I sat down and watched it with him. It showed men wearing helmets and talked a lot about casualties. I didn't understand much of it, but my parents assured me that it was far away, so I didn't concern myself with it.

◄○►

One day I came home from school to find a star in our window. I stopped outside and looked at it. My neighbor, who was watering his lawn, noticed and said, "That is to show that someone from your house is over fighting in Vietnam. You should be proud."

I wasn't sure what I had to be proud about, but after that, I was treated to extra cookies and snacks from many of the people on my block, so I didn't question it. I was trying to explain this special treatment to a friend of mine one day, saying how Mrs. Williams was good for a chocolate chip cookie if I just mentioned my brother Mark's name, when she interrupted me.

"Aren't you worried?" she asked.

I looked at her, puzzled. "Worried about what, eating too many cookies?"

"Worried that your brother might never come back," she explained.

It wasn't until I lay awake in bed that night that I realized what she meant. Never see my brother again? This was not something I wanted to think about. I wanted to stay sheltered. I wanted the adults to continue whispering in my presence. I wasn't ready to grow up, but it was too late.

Though I had already said my prayers with my mom when she tucked me in, I added a P.S.

Dear God,

I know that I have already asked you to bless the whole family, and that I said, "Amen," but if you could please give an extra blessing to my big brother I would appreciate it. I would like to get the chance to know him. In return, I promise not to eat any more of Mrs. Williams's chocolate chip cookies. At least until he comes back home. Amen.

The next morning Mom had to run some errands and asked if I wanted to go with her. Knowing I could wheedle at least an ice cream out of her on the way home, I normally would have jumped at the chance. This time I declined; I had a letter to write. She had been badgering me to write to my brother for some time, but I had always come up with one excuse or another.

My grades in spelling weren't the best, but I was sure Mark would be able to read it. I remembered he had once confided that he sometimes had trouble with spelling, too. After writing about school, some of the neighbors, and the latest trouble our sister had gotten into, I decided to draw a picture to go along with the letter. I drew him and me on a horse. He'd always loved horses and had promised to take me riding one day. I paused and then signed it: *I love you, Cindy.*

Had I ever told him that I loved him before?

I waited every day after that for the mail to come. Mom tried to explain that it could be weeks before Mark received my letter, let alone was able to reply. I wouldn't admit it, but I was afraid that maybe he wouldn't. My fears were unfounded, for he did write me back, and continued to answer every one of my letters until the day he finally came home.

We had a party that day in his honor. Besides family, the whole neighborhood turned out. Except for a hug when he first came in the door, I couldn't get near him. I wanted to talk to him, but there was a continuous crowd surrounding him. That evening, as the last of the well-wishers left, I watched him from the doorway. He was in the backyard sitting on the picnic table. He must've sensed my presence for he looked up and motioned for me to come outside. I suddenly felt shy.

Earlier in the day, someone had set up a radio outside for the welcome-home party, and now Mark turned it back on as I let the screen door bang behind me. With a flourish, he bowed slightly and held out his hand to me. "I believe you owe me a dance," he said. I couldn't help but giggle as I raced to him. My feet on his, we danced.

I've been a part of many homecomings in the more than thirty years since that one, but none as memorable.

The Small-Town Wave

by Lester Tucker | *Jesup, Georgia*

BORN AND RAISED IN SOUTH GEORGIA, small towns were all I knew in my youth. Inevitably, the small-town lifestyle is now forged into my being and, well, I like it that way.

Small towns have so many advantages that to name all of them would be impossible, but to give you a feel for what I'm talking about, I've included a few examples. For starters, you can leave your house five minutes before you have to be across town and still get there early. And then there's the reassurance of knowing all your neighbors. Though we do not have a neighborhood watch, everybody is aware of the comings and goings of everybody else, and we know we can rely on each other for help of any kind.

My mother and father, brother and family, and daughter and family all live nearby, and my twenty-year-old son lives at home. In fact, most of my family lives within a stone's throw and not many days go by that I don't see them. My grandsons probably cannot recall a day that we didn't see each other. That might be because my house seems to be the favorite gathering place, which could not delight me more. Of course the pool and pond play a big factor in it, but they are still content just to come and play with me. Although Grandmamma is loved, it is still referred to as Granddaddy's house, and she usually gets bypassed as they run to hug me upon arrival.

Because I retired four years ago at age forty-two, I've been able to enjoy much more time with my family. Bonds have been established with my grandchildren that will last a lifetime. Even they have started waving at people that pass by just because Granddaddy does.

In Jessup, our idea of a traffic jam is six or seven cars waiting for a train to pass, which always results in one or more drivers shutting off his or her car engine and getting out of the car to speak with others at the crossing. If the conversation is longer than the train, we just wave the passing cars around us. Sometimes that can result in drivers pulling up beside us and joining the conversation, thus blocking the road for a little longer. But nobody seems to mind. Everyone still waves as they pass—and they use all of their fingers. Road rage occurs only when walking barefoot on hot blacktop, in August, and lasts only until you reach the other side of the pavement. Even then you are usually laughing at yourself for the way you high-stepped it across the road.

I guess the best thing about small-town life is that no matter where you go, you will run into someone you know who wants to know how the family is doing. They ask because they care, and it's that caring that is the backbone of every small-town community. In a close-knit community you have a secure sense that everybody looks out for everybody. From the mayor to school bus drivers to firemen to doctors—we all know each other by first name. Those we don't know by name, we know by face.

Small towners are a right friendly bunch. We like to wave and beep our horns to people. It does not matter if they're in cars passing us, or whether we are driving or walking, or if we know them personally or not.

I feel it enlightens the soul not only to wave, but also to receive a wave back. I don't care where you are from, it won't take long driving in this area before you begin waving at cars as they pass. It's like a smile. The more you smile the more you notice others around you smiling.

But on a trip to Los Angeles a few months ago, I found out the hard way that this type of greeting is not universal. Fact is, some people use their car horns for reasons other than to acknowledge someone they know. After repeatedly turning around to wave, I soon learned horn beeping in the city has nothing to do with being nice. Some people did wave . . . with one finger.

I was only too happy to return home.

So, if you are ever traveling the back roads of south Georgia and pass through the town of Jesup and someone waves to you, please wave back. It could very well be me or my family or my friends, and every soul can use a little enlightening from time to time. ⤳

Be a part of the
Rocking Chair Reader series . . .

We hope you've enjoyed *Coming Home*, the flagship book in *The Rocking Chair Reader* series, as much as we've enjoyed bringing it to you. It goes without saying that those who lived or live in smalltown America have a story to tell that bears repeating, and we invite you to share yours with us for possible publication in future volumes of *The Rocking Chair Reader*.

When submitting to *The Rocking Chair Reader*, you may submit as many stories as you like. Please remember to include your name, address, phone number, and the name of the small town your story is written about.

Send all correspondence to *rockingchairreader@adamsmedia.com*.

If e-mail is not available, please snail mail to:

The Rocking Chair Reader
Adams Media
57 Littlefield Street
Avon, Massachusetts   02322

Current guidelines can be found at *www.rockingchairreader.com*.
Everyone has a story to tell, and we'd love to hear yours.

Contributors

Anna Abrams ("Water Witch"), born in 1911 to a newly emigrated homesteading family, today boasts of being a farmer, a mother, a sales clerk, a factory worker, an artist, a writer, a historian, and a traveler who has visited nearly every state in America, plus four foreign countries. She lives alone on her farm in Rupert, Idaho, still sharp-minded and fiercely independent. To her, family and heritage are everything.

Christy Lanier Attwood ("Another Way Home") resides in Austin, Texas, with her husband, Randy. Together, they have four wonderful children and a precious granddaughter. Christy graduated from St. Edward's University with a journalism degree. Writing is her lifelong passion. She is a contributor to *A Cup of Comfort for Christmas,* and has recently completed her first mystery novel, *Raw Deception.*

Gail Balden ("Can We Go Home Again?") is founder and director of Creative Journeys Writing Workshops for Women, an organization on the Oregon coast designed to bring women together to nurture their creative spirits and tell their stories. Her work has been published in *Oregon Coast* magazine, local journals and newspapers, and anthologies celebrating women's creativity, including: *Our Turn,*

Our Time, Women Truly Coming of Age; Midlife Clarity: Epiphanies from Grown-up Girls; and *A Cup of Comfort for Women.* She is currently working on a book about growing up in the small town of Dexter, Michigan. *www.creativejourneys.net.*

Sue A. Bentley ("A Mother's Love" and "Bed Check Charlie") currently is employed by the University of Michigan. She is new to the field of writing and is excited to be part of this book. She is working on a novel and booklet, and hopes to begin work next year on a cookbook. She enjoys traveling, reading, writing, and cooking.

Arthur Bowler ("A Dad and a Dog" and "Church on the Hill"), a U.S./Swiss citizen and graduate of Harvard Divinity School, is a writer and speaker in English and in German. His work has appeared in several bestselling inspirational anthologies. He is currently seeking representation for his book *A Prayer and a Swear.* Contact him at *www.arthurbowler.ch.*

Kelley Kay Bowles ("This Town, My Home") is an English and drama teacher in Grand Junction, Colorado. Her work has been published in several inspirational anthologies. She recently received her MFA in creative writing and is searching for an agent for two completed mystery novels as she works on her first young adult novel.

Lanita Bradley Boyd ("Rotary Club Pianist") is a freelance writer in Fort Thomas, Kentucky. In her writing, she draws from years of teaching, church ministry, and family experiences. She has stories in several inspirational anthologies, and articles in a variety of publications, including *Teaching K-8, Christian Woman,* and *Parent Life.*

Mary Ralph Bradley ("Sleeping at the Foot of the Bed") has been a teacher, Gallup pollster, legal office secretary and manager, farmer, politician, operator of a bed-and-breakfast, and homemaker. She is the author of *Memories, Mysteries, and Musings.* Her Tennessee home, Ajalon Acres, is a haven for the downtrodden—some for hours, others for years. Above all, she honors God and teaches the good news of Jesus Christ.

Sylvia Bright-Green ("Down the Lane of My Sweet Memories") is a seasoned writer with more than 500 articles, photo-features, columns, and short stories published in local and national publications. Green has also coauthored a county historical book, taught writing classes at the University of Wisconsin Centers, hosted a cable talk show, and served as the local and state writers' president.

Marcia E. Brown ("The Grape Jelly Lady") of Austin, Texas, writes of her Depression Era childhood in Oklahoma and Arkansas to preserve family stories for her son and cousins. Since 1993, her work has appeared regularly in magazines, newspapers, and anthologies, including the *A Cup of Comfort* series.

Stephanie Ray Brown ("All-Star Washer Player") lives in Henderson, Kentucky. She is blessed to be Terry's wife, Savannah and Cameron's mother, Rita's daughter, and, of course, Uncle David's niece. Although she no longer lives near those Webster County cornfields, she will always consider that home.

Renie Burghardt ("The Green Stamp Heirloom"), who was born in Hungary, is a freelance writer with many credits. She has contributed to various inspirational anthologies, a dozen *Guideposts* books, and many others. She lives in the country and loves nature, animals, gardening, reading, and spending time with family and friends.

Barbara J. Burk ("Roy Rogers and the Tent Show"), the eldest of eight children and mother of three, was born and raised in the Missouri Ozarks. She currently resides in Nashville, Tennessee, and is the patient services coordinator and systems administrator for The Leukemia and Lymphoma Society's Tennessee chapter. She loves writing, reading, drama, and hiking.

Michele Wallace Campanelli ("The Rag Man") is a national bestselling author. Her work has been published in various anthologies and she has penned many novels, including *Keeper of the Shroud* and *Margarita*. Lauretta Pauline, Michele's grandmother, shared this memory with her. Visit her at *www.michelecampanelli.com*.

Nan B. Clark ("Swimming for St. Peter"), who once lived on Pavilion Beach herself, has connections to Gloucester, Massachusetts, that are deep and passionate. She married her husband, Tom, there, and for many years has been a guide at Beauport, a museum on the harbor, where she met the woman who shared this story with her.

Jamie Cope ("Uncle Ben") prides himself on creating stories that appeal to all ages. Through his company, Destiny Images, Jamie has created numerous children's television programs, such as the award-winning *Letter* TV series. Jamie lives in Scott Depot, West Virginia, and enjoys spending time with his wife, Amy, and their two kids, Hannah and Noah. He maintains professional status in the Society of Children's Writers and Illustrators, and his story "Noah: The Ordinary Goldfish" was a winner of the 2003 West Virginia Writers, Inc., competition.

Barbara Davey ("Legacy in a Soup Pot") is an executive director at Christ Hospital in Jersey City, New Jersey, where she is responsible for marketing, public relations, and fund-raising. Her short stories and essays have been published in various anthologies, including *A Cup of Comfort*. She is a graduate of Seton Hall University, where she received her master's degree in English and education. Her motto in life is: "Expect a miracle, and you will probably receive one!" She and her husband, Reinhold Becker, live in Verona, New Jersey, where they patronize many restaurants featuring takeout, as neither has any mastery of culinary skills. She may be reached at *wise words2@aol.com*.

Jean Davidson ("The Great Potato Patch"), former administrative assistant, took early retirement several years ago and is now a full-time student at Idaho State University in Pocatello, Idaho. She enjoys studying whatever piques her interest and claims her greatest passions are being with her family and writing their stories.

Bob Davis ("Grandma's Cookie Jar") spent thirty years as a historian for the U.S. Air Force, retiring in August 2002 as a Chief Master Sergeant, the highest enlisted grade. He currently resides in San Antonio, Texas, where he's working on his first novel. He and his wife have been married thirty-two years and have three grown children and two grandchildren.

Betty Downs ("Sugar Cookies and Quilts") is the widow of a road construction mechanic. The mother of four sons, five grandchildren, and two step-grandchildren, Betty lives in the beautiful Black Hills of South Dakota. She enjoys traveling, writing, and playing in her flower garden.

Sandy Williams Driver ("Love at First Sight" and "The Redbirds") lives in Albertville, Alabama, with her husband, Tim, and their children, Josh, Jake, and Katie. She is a full-time homemaker and a part-time writer with stories published in magazines all over the world. She also writes a weekly parenting column for her local newspaper, *The Sand Mountain Reporter.*

Margaret A. Frey ("Circles of Fire") started her career as a copy/production editor in Philadelphia, Pennsylvania. Her early work was published in *Asphodel.* More recently, her fiction has been published in *Literary Potpourri, Bovine Free Wyoming, Flashquake, Wild Strawberries,* and elsewhere. Margaret's nonfiction has appeared in *Writer's Digest* and her human-interest piece, "Skipping Stones," took second place in the 2003 Erma Bombeck writing competition. She lives and writes from the foothills of the Smoky Mountains with her husband, and canine literary critic, Ruffian.

Heather Froeschl ("Across the Bay") is the author of thirteen books and hard at work on several more. She is a freelance editor working with numerous authors and publishers. She lives happily in the Blue Ridge Mountains with her family and way too many pets. Visit her Web page to learn more: *www.Quilldipper.com.*

Shirley P. Gumert ("Friendship Interrupted") is a freelance writer and regular contributor to *Texas* magazine, a Sunday supplement to *The Houston Chronicle.* She was formerly a columnist for *The Santa Fe Reporter,* where, in the 1980s, she won state and national awards. She also has written for several other New Mexico and Texas newspapers and magazines.

Nancy Gustafson ("The Bricks of Fort Scott") has published poetry, short fiction, and articles in anthologies and journals, including *A Cup of Comfort for Inspiration, Suddenly IV* and *Suddenly V, Lucidity Poetry Journal, Inner Visions, The Herbalist's Journal, The MAADvocate, Banshee Studios* magazine (e-zine: bansheestudios.net), and several *Poetry Society of Texas Books of the Year.* She is retired from Sam Houston State University, where she worked as a program coordinator for the Correctional Management Institute of Texas at the George J. Beto Criminal Justice Center. She lives in Huntsville, Texas.

Linda Henson ("The Macramé Curtains") has had stories published in Christian magazines and various anthologies. She lives in the Bahamas, where she presently is administrator/teacher of Abaco Bible College. She also writes for a local newspaper, and is a counselor, musician, and former language arts teacher. *ernie.henson@ agmd.org*

Marie D. Jones ("The Old Lady's Field") now lives in Southern California—although her heart resides in Garnerville, and always will. She is a widely published writer, progressive activist, and mom. Her latest book is titled *Looking for God in All the Wrong Places*. She still believes in the Old Lady.

Mary (Szymanski) Koss ("I Came Home to Say Goodbye") is a lifelong resident of Northern Michigan, where she is manager/CEO of the Alpena County Medical Credit Union. While new to creative writing, Mary is an avid reader. Her family is her foundation and source of inspiration. She and her husband, Gene, are the proud parents of four children, Annah, Emmy, Nicholas, and Eric, and equally as proud of their adorable grandchildren, Abigail and Bobby.

Polly Camp Kreitz ("A Plank Is the Deed to My Memories") is published in several inspirational anthologies. She also has completed her first novel, *Magnolia Meadows*, and has a second novel, *Hollyhock Ridge*, in progress. Both novels are set in Alabama.

Suzanne LaFetra ("Last Leg of the Journey") is a freelance writer and columnist living in the San Francisco Bay Area.

Sharon Landeen ("The Girl in Charge") is a retired elementary teacher. She keeps busy with grandchildren and enjoys working with youth through the reading programs she offers in local schools, and as a 4-H leader. She has written and illustrated two bilingual picture books, and has been published in various adult and children's magazines, and inspirational anthology books.

Steven Manchester ("A Promise") is the father of two sons. He also is the published author of *The Unexpected Storm: The Gulf War Legacy, Jacob Evans, A Father's Love,* and *At the Stroke of Midnight,* as well as several books under the pseudonym Steven Herberts. His work has been showcased in such national literary journals as *Taproot Literary Review, American Poetry Review,* and *Fresh!* literary magazine. He is an accomplished speaker and currently teaches the popular workshop Write a Book, Get Published & Promote Your Work. Three of his screenplays have been produced as films. When not spending time with his sons, writing, teaching, or promoting his work, he speaks publicly to troubled children through the "Straight Ahead" program.

Claudia McCormick ("Tea for Three") is a published writer. Her work has appeared in various inspirational anthologies. She also wrote a newspaper column for more than ten years, and currently is serving as the vice mayor of her town.

Loretta Miller Mehl ("Letting Go") crafts stories about her life as a sharecropper's child. She also writes about the people she loves: her husband of fifty-five years Bill, four children, thirteen gifted grandchildren, and her friends. Former secretary for the City of San

Marino, California, she now resides in Eugene, Oregon. She is a Sunday school teacher and is interested in gardening and people.

Lynn Ruth Miller ("Forty Birkhead Place") has published several hundred stories and feature articles throughout the country. Her current column, "Thoughts While Walking the Dog," is a regular holiday feature in *The Pacifica Tribune*. In addition to her autobiographical novel, *Starving Hearts*, she has compiled and published several of her essays as books: *Thoughts While Walking the Dog* and *More Thoughts While Walking the Dog*. She also has an audio CD titled *Thoughts and More Thoughts*. She hosts two public access television programs: Channel 26 in Pacifica, "What's Hot Between the Covers" (book reviews and interviews in the arts), and "Paint with Lynn" (a hands-on creative arts series). Her stories have been included in three volumes of *A Cup of Comfort*.

Lad Moore ("Single Vision") lives on a small farm near historic Jefferson, Texas. His work has been published both in print and on the Internet more than 400 times. Two of his collections, *Odie Dodie* and *Tailwind*, are currently available at major booksellers.

Denise Carlson Nash ("A Chronicle of Unexpected Blessings") and her husband live on Oregon's scenic McKenzie River, where they both grew up. She is an emergency department RN, and writes part time.

Sylvia Nickels ("Persimmon Memories") lives in northeast Tennessee. Her stories and nostalgic essays on growing up in rural Georgia have been published online and in print.

Rhoda Novak ("Where I Belong") and John, her husband and college lab partner, are innovators in the aerospace industry in

Southern California. In addition to engineering and mentoring other women engineers, she studies creative writing. Her award-winning work is published in poetry journals, anthologies, newspapers, engineering journals, and Web lit magazines. She enjoys weekly visits with her daughter, Jennifer, and grandson Matthew, time with John, and frequent phone calls to Momma.

CJ Nyman ("Home Sweet Home") is a member of the South Carolina Writers group. Her story is set in the hills of Felton, California, a small town just miles from Santa Cruz.

Sharon Cupp Pennington ("Another Summer's End") resides in Texas and is presently working on her first romantic suspense novel, *Hoodoo Money*. Her short stories have been published in *The Emporium Gazette, The Written Wisdom, Seasons for Writing, FlashQuake, Mocha Memoirs,* and *Flash Shots*. She can be reached via e-mail at *sepen2@express56.com*.

Linda Kaullen Perkins ("Shopping Spree") has published articles in the local newspaper, *The Standard; Living,* a Virginia publication; and *Country Woman*. Over the past seven years, she has contributed short stories to *Party Line,* a local magazine. She retired in 2001—after thirty-one years as an elementary teacher—and since has completed a 70,000-word historical manuscript.

Kimberly A. Porrazzo ("See the USA") is a senior writer for *OC Metro* and *OC Family* magazines in Southern California. For the past five years she has written a column called "Mother Knows." In 2002, she was honored with the silver award for her column by the Parenting Publications Association of America. She is the author of *The Nanny Kit,* and has been published in an inspirational anthology.

Carol McAdoo Rehme ("Christmas Pet") is a freelance writer and editor. She publishes prolifically in the inspirational market. She also coauthored three books in 2003: *Angels Watching Over Us, Angels Book,* and *Journal, Blessings Book and Journal.*

Lois Larrance Requist ("The Ditch Rider") writes a senior column at *www.benicianews.com* and has published poetry, fiction—one novel—and various short stories, as well as nonfiction articles on travel, and additional pieces. She has a BA and MA in English with an emphasis on creative writing from San Francisco State University. She is a traveler, writer, grandmother, and all-around active person.

Roberta Rhodes ("State Route 149") was born on a farm in Iowa during the difficult Depression years. When she was four years old, her family moved to Wyoming, leaving behind one little farm community, two sets of grandparents, and a profusion of aunts, uncles, and cousins. Most summers found her back on the farm, soaking up love and storing up memories. She now lives and writes in Pennsylvania and has been published in *Birds & Blooms, Mature Living,* and other magazines. She also writes a monthly column for *Tri-State Senior News* in Erie, Pennsylvania, and is an occasional contributor to the *Erie Pennsylvania Times/News.*

Cindy Robert ("A Prayer for My Brother") has had stories published in *Women's World, Grit,* and various anthologies. She lives in Florida with her husband, three children, and an assortment of animals.

Leigh Platt Rogers ("Song at Sunrise") was raised all over the world by virtue of her father's occupation (CIA). An avid writer, she has been published in *Spies Wives,* several inspirational anthologies, as well as *BookBanter.com* and *The Yarrow Brook Literary Review.* Her book *Sticky Situations: Stories of Childhood Adventures Abroad* is now available. Visit her Web site at *www.leighplattrogers.com*.

Stephen D. Rogers ("The Town Dump") is the author of more than 300 essays, stories, and poems, which have been selected to appear in more than 100 publications. Although he resides on the Web at *www.stephendrogers.com*, he still considers Holliston home.

Bob Rose ("Home Again") and his wife, Kathy, have been married for twenty-nine years. They have three sons, two daughters-in-law, and five grandchildren. He has worked in many fields, including the academic world as a music and drama teacher, and also as a chef, salesman, counselor, and, currently, pastor to the only church in Sinclair, Wyoming. His publication credits include magazines such as *Home Life, Experiencing God, The Christian Communicator, Ideals,* and *Church Libraries.* He also has written a weekly newspaper column, "Crossed Paths," since 1995, which has appeared in numerous Texas newspapers and currently runs in the Rawlins, Wyoming, *Daily Times.*

Mary Norton Ross ("Home Harbor") As a child of World War II, Mary attended twelve different schools in whatever part of the country the Navy sent her father. In complete contrast, her parents grew up in a small town in New England where their forebearers for centuries are buried. It was this town of Wallingford, Connecticut, to which she came home.

Elaine Ernst Schneider ("Granny's Garden Hat") is a freelance writer who has published articles, songs, and children's work. Her work has appeared in *Catholic Digest, FellowScript, Parenting Today's Teen, This Christian Life, HomeLearning Canada, Cup of Comfort for*

Mothers and Daughters, and *Whispers from Heaven.* Presently, Elaine is a freelance curriculum author for Group Publishing, Inc., and the managing editor of the Web site Lesson Tutor.

Lori Z. Scott ("The Heart of the River") lives in Terre Haute, Indiana, with her husband and two children. Some of her publications include author contributions to *Real Moms* and *A Cup of Comfort Devotional.* She cherishes her own memories of Indian River and is still waiting to catch a rainbow.

Cindy Emmet Smith ("Return to the Lamb") lives in central Pennsylvania with her husband and three children. She currently is a member of St. David's Christian Writers' Association and West Branch Christian Writers and has published one novel, *The Cracked and Silent Mirror.* Her most recently published work is a short story that appeared in the April 2003 issue of *True Confessions.* She contributes regularly to *Time of Singing* and has had worship services appear in *Church Worship* magazine.

Joyce Stark ("Passing Strangers") lives in northeast Scotland. She and her husband have traveled widely in North America and Europe. Joyce writes for various magazines and anthologies in the United States and the United Kingdom. Her ambition is to earn enough money from writing to make a career of visiting small-town America.

Michele (Shelly) Starkey ("When a Second Takes Forever") is a brain aneurysm survivor who enjoys writing and sharing her stories. She is living life to the fullest with her husband, Keith, in the Hudson Valley of New York State.

Wade A. Stevenson ("A Special Cup of Coffee") is a retired special agent from the U.S. Department of Defense Investigative

Service, and author of the nationwide bestselling novel *The Salzdorf Wellspring.* His most recently completed novel, *Mountains Prime Evil,* was released in late 2003.

David Crane Swarts ("The Pilot and the Paperboy") received his education at Rushville Consolidated High School, and received his BSME at Duke University. He is a Registered Professional Engineer (PE) in Illinois and Indiana, and lived in the Chicago, Illinois, area from 1972 to 1996. He returned to Fort Wayne, Indiana, in 1996. He is the father of two sons, Zachary, seven, and Daniel, four.

Annemarieke Tazelaar ("Changing Hearths") was born in the Netherlands but moved to Michigan with her family after World War II. She was a teacher for twenty years and currently owns her own business. She spends her spare time writing. Several of her articles appear in the *A Cup of Comfort* series.

Lester Tucker ("The Small-Town Wave") was born in 1956 in Tifton, Georgia. He and his wife, Sandra, have been married for twenty-five years. Lester has been writing since elementary school and has a passion for the literary arts. He enjoys retirement and spending time with his family.

Peggy Vincent ("The Soldier in the Gold Frame"), a retired midwife, is the author of *Baby Catcher: Chronicles of a Modern Midwife,* a memoir. Her many essays and articles have appeared in a wide variety of publications, including *Reader's Digest, Christian Science Monitor, Skirt!,* and *Bird Watcher's Digest.* Now retired, she lives in California with her husband and teenage son.

Garnet Hunt White ("The Power of Oma's Popcorn") taught school and also booked movies for Garrett and Oma Hunt's Hunt

Theatre. She loved bargaining with the children by exchanging popcorn for movie seats. Garnet loves pets and helps abused animals.

Janet Shaub White ("Gatherings Remembered") lives in south-central Wisconsin, where the glaciated landscape and clear lakes are easy on the eyes and soothing to one's disposition. She has taught three-year-olds through adults, operated a floral design business, done interior decorating, written curriculum and newspaper columns, taught writing and editing, and volunteered at school and church. She is mom to two grown sons. Today, she works part-time so that there will be a few hours more each week in which to write.

Gay Wiggin-Comboy ("Home Is Where Mama Is") was born the eleventh of twelve children on a large dairy farm in northwest Arkansas. After her father died in 1951, the family moved into the small town of Gravette. She is retired from AT&T and lives with her husband, Joe, in Independence, Missouri. She keeps busy with antiquing, crafts, traveling, helping her aunt, and playing with her great-nieces.

Leslie J. Wyatt ("Kentucky Girl") is a freelance writer. Her work has been accepted for publication by several anthologies, including *A Cup of Comfort for Courage*, *My Heart's First Steps*, and *Yahweh Sisterhood*. In addition to numerous published articles and stories, and business writing, her middle-grade historical novel is under contract with Holiday House.

About the Editor

HELEN KAY POLASKI has always believed in magic, especially the kind that keeps marriages together, binds siblings and friends, and ties the concept of home close to the heart. She is the seventh child in a family of sixteen children and hails from a small town in northern Michigan, near the shores of Lake Huron, where she met and married her high school sweetheart.

After seventeen years as a newspaper reporter/photographer and editor, she left her full-time job to follow her dream of becoming a book author. In the past four years, she has worn many hats, including book author, book editor, storyteller, essayist, journalist, poet, book and movie reviewer, songwriter, graphic artist, and copresident of the Southeast Michigan Writers' Association. When not on the computer, she is busy exploring the world with her husband and three children, and is pleased to say most trips still take her back to Metz, Michigan, where she was born and raised, and where the magic is strongest.